RESEARCH MONOGRAPH OF THE NATIONAL ASSOCIATION
FOR THE EDUCATION OF YOUNG CHILDREN, VOLUME 5

Family Day Care:
Out of the Shadows and Into the Limelight

Ministry of Education, Ontario
Information Services
13th Floor, Mowat Block, Queen's Park
Toronto M7A 1L2

Susan Kontos

A 1991–92 NAEYC Comprehensive Membership benefit

National Association for the Education of Young Children
Washington, DC

FOR LOU AND WYNNE

Photo credits: Francis Wardle, p. 2; David Halsey, pp. 9, 15, 87; Richard Myers-Walls, pp. 20, 53, 75; © Cleo Freelance Photo, p. 28; Skjold Photographs, p. 37; Nancy P. Alexander, pp. 41, 105; The Growth Program, pp. 44, 49, 80, 92; Ellen Galinsky, p. 60; Subjects & Predicates, pp. 65, 69, 100, 131, 141; © A.S. Haase, p. 97; © Rick Reinhard, p. 108; Elisabeth Nichols, p. 115; © Bm Porter 1992/Don Franklin, p. 120; Michael D. Sullivan, p. 136; Jeffrey High Image Productions, p. 149.

Copyright © 1992 by Susan Kontos. All rights reserved.

National Association for the Education of Young Children
1834 Connecticut Avenue, N.W.
Washington, DC 20009–5786

The National Association for the Education of Young Children attempts through its publications program to provide a forum for discussion of major issues and ideas in our field. We hope to provoke thought and promote professional growth. The views expressed or implied are not necessarily those of the Association.

Library of Congress Catalog Number: 92–060002

ISBN Catalog Number: 0–935989–50–1

NAEYC #144

Editor: Polly Greenberg; *Book design and production:* Jack Zibulsky; *Copyediting and proofreading:* Penny Atkins and Betty Nylund Barr; *Editorial assistance:* Julie Andrews

Printed in the United States of America.

Contents

Acknowledgments ... vi

1. Introduction ... 1
    What is family day care? ... 3
    Supply and demand: How does family day care fit into the child care "marketplace?" ... 3
    Issues and themes: What do we need to know about family day care? ... 8

2. The Ecology of Family Day Care ... 13
    Activities: What do children and caregivers do? ... 14
        Summary ... 18
    How are caregiver behaviors related to caregiver characteristics and conditions of caregiving? ... 19
        Caregiver characteristics ... 19
        Conditions of caregiving ... 21
        Summary ... 23
    Relationship of caregiver characteristics and behavior and conditions of caregiving to children's behavior and development ... 23
        Caregiver characteristics ... 23
        Caregiver behavior ... 24
        Conditions of caregiving ... 26
        Summary ... 27
    Relationship of family day care quality to children's behavior and development ... 28
    Family factors as moderators of family day care quality influences on children ... 31
    Summary and implications ... 33

3. Characteristics of Caregivers: Who Are They? ... 35
    National Day Care Home Study ... 35
    Personal characteristics ... 38
        Age ... 38
        Marital status ... 38

   Family size . . . 39
   Education . . . 39
   Income . . . 40
   Social support . . . 43
  Professional characteristics . . . 46
   Experience . . . 46
   Training . . . 47
   Motivation . . . 51
   Job satisfaction . . . 52
   Job commitment . . . 55
  Summary . . . 57
   Implications . . . 58

4. What Services Do Family Day Care Providers Provide? . . . 59
  Number of children in care . . . 59
  Fees . . . 62
  Work hours . . . 63
  Planning and organization . . . 64
  Quality . . . 67
  Summary . . . 70
   Implications . . . 70

5. Families That Use Family Day Care . . . 73
  Who are the families? . . . 74
   Socioeconomic status . . . 74
   Satisfaction with care . . . 75
   Likes and dislikes . . . 76
   Selection of family day care . . . 78
  Parent/caregiver relationships . . . 83
   Communication . . . 83
   Conflict . . . 86
   Duration . . . 89
  Summary . . . 89
   Implications . . . 90

6. Licensing and Accreditation . . . 91
  Regulation . . . 93
   Types of regulation . . . 93
   What is regulated . . . 94

Future directions for family day care regulation . . . 96
Caregivers' views of regulation . . . 103
Summary . . . 109
Accreditation . . . 110
  CDA Family Day Care credential . . . 110
  NAFDC accreditation . . . 112
  Comparison of accreditation programs . . . 114
  Impact of accreditation . . . 116
Summary . . . 118

7. Training . . . 119
Looking at successful components of training programs . . . 121
  Training format . . . 121
  Training intensity . . . 130
  Training content . . . 132
Effects of training . . . 132
  Satisfaction with/helpfulness of training . . . 133
  Knowledge and attitudes . . . 133
  Quality of child care . . . 135
  Caregiver behavior . . . 137
  Retention . . . 139
What does training predict? . . . 141
Barriers to training: Motivation and recruitment . . . 143
Summary . . . 145
Implications . . . 146

8. Issues and Themes Revisited: Looking to the Future . . . 147
What do we know? . . . 147
Longevity/turnover . . . 148
Child care as family support . . . 152
Regulation . . . 153
Training and professionalism . . . 154
Quality . . . 155
Compensation and affordability . . . 157
Looking to the future . . . 158

References . . . 160
Index . . . 168
Information About NAEYC . . . Cover 3

Acknowledgments

THIS MONOGRAPH WAS COMPLETED WITH the assistance of a number of people. Carollee Howes, Johanna Nicholas, and Kathy Modigliani critically reviewed several chapters in their early stages. A number of anonymous reviewers provided thoughtful comments on the manuscript. Feedback from these various sources was incorporated in the final version of the monograph.

When the work on this project was initiated, Pat Broker spent many hours in the library gathering the readings and organizing them by content. Becky Harshman took on the formidable task of typing the table in Chapter 7, and Karen Devenish typed the reference list. Denise Cady provided quality family day care for my daughter while I worked on the manuscript.

I wish to express my appreciation to each of these people for their contribution to my work.

Chapter 1

Introduction

IN THE POST-REAGAN ERA of privatized funding and reduced governmental regulation, it is no coincidence that family day care is getting more attention. Compared to child care centers, family day care is highly privatized in its funding and more likely to elude (not always intentionally) governmental regulation. Family day care also allows women who so choose to stay home with their children while earning an income (Nelson, 1988). A general surge of interest in child care issues may partly account for this increase in attention being paid to family day care, a form of child care that has typically operated in the shadows of its more visible (if less used) cousin—center-based care. Thus, policymakers who may have been skeptical about child care in the past can confidently join the countless families who, for years, have gravitated toward family day care as their children's "home away from home" while the parents work.

An even more important factor moving family day care out of the shadows and into the child care limelight is the array of state and national programs initiated recently that are aimed at recruitment and retention of caregivers as well as improving the quality of family day care (e.g., California Child Care Resource and Referral Network, 1988; Cohen, 1990; Cohen & Modigliani, 1990; National Center for Children in Poverty, 1991). These initiatives are improving the image of family day care, have given a new vitality to the field, and give needed recognition and support to family day care providers (Adams, 1989).

Another result of recent family day care initiatives is greater need for a solid knowledge base about family day care, assuming such knowledge will enhance the development and effectiveness of programs for family day care providers. This need has gone largely unfulfilled recently because it has been some time since anyone has published a comprehensive review of research on the subject (Wattenberg, 1980; Raven, 1981). The prime purpose of this volume is to examine what research studies can tell us about family day care, drawing implications for practice as well as providing recommendations for the direction of future research on the subject.

Is there really a family day care knowledge base? The literature on family day care is replete with statements regarding its popularity with parents contrasted with its neglect by researchers. There is no question that family day care has been the most frequently used form of out-of-home child care

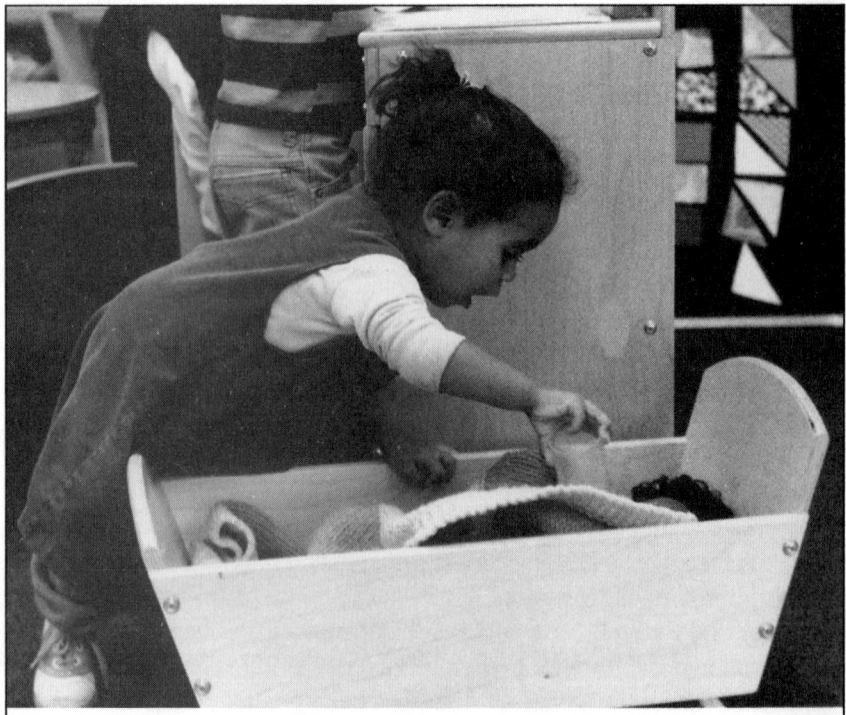

The most recent family day care licensing study found that there were 223,351 regulated family day care homes in the United States. Experts estimate that there are over five million children in family day care in this country and that unregulated providers represent 60% to 90% of the total population of providers.

(Hofferth & Phillips, 1987; Kahn & Kamerman, 1987), although recently the numbers are dropping off for mothers who work full-time or have children over three years of age. The claim of neglect by researchers, however, may have been overstated. Even though center-based child care has been more heavily researched, family day care (in particular, regulated family day care) has been far from ignored. One reason the research on family day care has been less visible is that the results have not always been disseminated through traditional scholarly sources. Nonetheless, taken as a whole, the literature on family day care is more extensive than many individuals have presumed, even if research has not been equally distributed across topics nor disseminated in scholarly journals. It is time for a comprehensive review of family day care research.

What is family day care?

Family day care is typically defined as a child care arrangement in which up to six children are cared for in the home of a nonrelative (Children's Foundation, 1989). Usually, the caregiver's own preschool children are counted as part of the group and, in some states, the maximum allowable group size is contingent on the ages of the children. In some states (12), the maximum number of children allowed for one caregiver is greater than six (7 to 12); in many states (36), homes with more than six children are required to have a second adult present and are called *group homes* or *large family day care homes*.

Supply and demand: How does family day care fit into the child care "marketplace?"

The most recent family day care licensing study found that there were 223,351 regulated family day care homes (including group homes) in the United States (Children's Foundation, 1990). This number is based on state lists of regulated family day care providers. Because not all caregivers on these lists are actually providing care, this number is typically a bit inflated. According to *A Profile of Child Care Settings* (PCS [Willer, Hofferth, Kisker, Divine-Hawkins, Farquhar, & Glantz, 1991]), there are approximately 118,000 operating regulated family day care providers. The number of unregulated family day care homes is more difficult to verify because there is no mechanism for counting them; only estimates are available. These estimates are based on extrapolations of known statistics, such as the number of children who need child care, the number of children in center-based care and in-home or relative care, and the average number of children per family day care home. Kahn and Kamerman (1987) estimated that there are just over five million children in family day care in the United States. Unregulated caregivers represent 60% to 90% of the total population of providers. If the average number of children per home is three to three-and-one-half, then we can estimate that the total number of family day care providers ranges from between one-and-one-half million to two million family day care providers (Kahn & Kamerman, 1986; Hofferth & Phillips, 1987). More recent estimates based on the PCS (Willer et al., 1991) suggest that there are fewer unregulated caregivers (550,000 to 1.1 million).

Whether this supply of family day care providers meets the parental demand for them is anybody's guess. According to Hofferth and Phillips (1991), ample licensed child care slots are available for preschool children needing care. In fact, Hofferth and Phillips' calculations show that the child care supply outstrips the demand nationally. If supply and demand problems exist, they are likely to be local shortages. These shortages may be specific to type of care (center- versus home-based), age of the child (e.g., infant and after-school care), regulatory status, cost, and quality. Thus, in spite of the national availability of child care, a number of factors may be contributing to shortages within a given geographic area.

Glantz (1989) believes that the supply of family day care in a particular community is tied to the community's employment options for women. Women who can earn higher salaries in other jobs are less likely to provide child care. Thus, in low-income or working-class neighborhoods, the supply of family day care is likely to be high, while the demand, due to the lack of lucrative employment alternatives, is likely to be relatively low. Glantz hypothesizes that the reverse will be true in middle- and upper-income neighborhoods. The results of the National Child Care Supply and Needs

There is no question that family day care has been the most frequently used form of out-of-home child care, although recently the numbers are dropping off for mothers who work full-time or have children over three years of age.

Study (Kisker, Maynard, Gordon, & Strain, 1989), conducted in three urban, blue-collar areas, supported Glantz's views. Family day care in these three communities was underused.

Which families are gravitating toward family day care? Two groups stand out: families in which mothers are employed part-time and families with children under the age of three. Increases in usage of family day care by these two groups accounts for the modest increase in overall use of family day care between 1965 and 1982 (Hofferth & Phillips, 1987). Thirty-six percent of the children served in family day care are under the age of three. In 1990 (Bureau of the Census, 1990; Hofferth & Brayfield, 1991), family day care homes served 20% of all preschool children of employed mothers (nearly equal to the percentage who use care by relatives). Twenty-eight percent of the preschool children of employed mothers were in center-based programs. Current projections on child care usage indicate that use of family day care is increasing at a slower rate than the use of center-based care (Hofferth & Phillips, 1987). Presently, it is difficult to determine whether this trend reflects parental preferences or the changing availability of services; both explanations may be valid.

The familiarity of the home setting, more flexible hours, affordability, and the convenience of a neighborhood location are frequently cited as reasons for the widespread use of family day care. Child care consumer surveys confirming these reasons are scarce. Some empirical evidence suggests that family day care offers more flexible hours. Using a sample of welfare mothers, Sonenstein and Wolf (1991) found that, similar to care by relatives in their home, family day care was more likely than center-based care or in-home care to serve children before 7 A.M. and after 6 P.M. In that same study, family day care and out-of-home care by relatives were perceived by mothers to be more inconveniently located than other forms of care. Consistent with these perceptions, Canadian parents using family day care reported that they lived farther away from their caregivers (12.3 km.) than did parents using center-based care (7.7 km.) (Kivikink & Schell, 1987). Thus, the image of family day care as a convenient neighborhood child care option may be less accurate than its image of flexibility of hours. Choice of child care may be based on other criteria.

Choice of child care is thought to reflect the type of care that parents prefer for their children. Kamerman and Kahn (1981), however, found that the reverse may be true; parents tend to prefer whatever mode of child care they

Many parents say that they prefer parent or relative care for children younger than age three and center-based care for four- and five-year-olds.

are currently using and are satisfied with. In spite of this fact, it is also true that significant numbers of parents would like to change from family day care to either center-based care or care in the child's own home (Kamerman & Kahn, 1981; Fuqua & Schieck, 1989). Only 40% of the parents in a study of "childminding" in Britain initially preferred a "minder" (Bryant, Harris, & Newton, 1980), and only three to five percent of Detroit parents perceived of family day care as the ideal child care arrangement for a young child with an employed mother (Mason & Kuhlthau, 1989).

Examining the preference data by form of care currently used, the National Child Care Supply and Needs Study (Kisker et al., 1989) found that the majority of family day care users (62% to 74%) desired no change in child care arrangements, but users who did want to change tended to prefer a center-based program. It was rare for parents using center-based care to want to change to family day care. Kisker et al. found that, of the parents desiring a change in their child care arrangements (27% to 32% of the total parent sample, depending on locale), few preferred family day care (only 4% to 11%). These data suggest that perhaps the widespread use of family day care is more a reflection of availability than of preference.

On the other hand, it is also true that parents increasingly prefer center-based care for their children as they approach two-and-a-half to three years of age (Fuqua & Labensohn, 1986; Kahn & Kamerman, 1987); thus, a desire to change from family day care to center-based care could be an accommodation to children's developmental status rather than an indication of dissatisfaction with family day care. When mothers of preschool children were asked what they considered the ideal form of child care when mothers are employed, their responses varied according to the age of their child (Mason & Kuhlthau, 1989). Center-based care was perceived as ideal for four- and five-year-olds, whereas parent or relative care was perceived as ideal for younger preschoolers. Family day care was not considered an ideal form of child care for children of any age. Overall, we can probably surmise that parents of three- to five-year-olds are less likely to use family day care as a matter of preference.

Recent studies show that the economics of child care is a major factor in its selection. Sonenstein and Wolf (1991) found that only 62% of the welfare mothers in their study who used family day care paid for it. Of those who did pay, the cost of care was rated as significantly more unreasonable than other forms of care, especially center-based care. Perceptions of how reasonable the

Family day care clearly has a solid role in the child care marketplace. Its most loyal customers are mothers of infants and toddlers and mothers who work part-time.

cost of care was were unrelated to actual reported costs. In fact, the most expensive child care option, in-home sitters, was reported to be the most reasonable. Out-of-pocket expense clearly was not the determining factor in perceptions of "reasonableness" of cost. Although these results appear to be illogical, perhaps parents' notions of reasonable costs are related to their preferences for type of child care (i.e., it may seem "reasonable" to pay more for a preferred form of care). Recent research shows that family day care is comparable in cost to center-based care, thus negating affordability as an advantage of family day care (Kivikink & Schell, 1987; Kisker et al., 1989; Hayes, Palmer, & Zaslow, 1990; Hofferth & Wissoker, 1990).

Using the 1985 sample of the National Longitudinal Survey of Youth, Hofferth and Wissoker (1990) estimated the impact of price, quality, family income, and family characteristics on choice of four modes of child care: center, sitter, relative, and husband/partner. Unfortunately, the sitter care category did not distinguish between care given in the child's home versus in the sitter's home, but the sample included more families using care in the sitter's home. Thus, this study provides us with tentative data regarding who chooses what forms of child care. The parents in this sample reported spending between $30 and $42 per week for child care. The costs reported for family day care and center-based care were approximately equivalent. Families in the South were less likely to choose sitter care than center-based care, reflecting a regional difference in taste. Parents typically chose the least expensive form of care available to them. Quality, as measured by adult-child ratio, did not affect parents' selection of family day care, although it did for the selection of center-based care. When maternal (not family) earnings were higher, center-based care was more likely to be selected. Overall, these data suggested that price and mothers' earnings were the two most important determinants of parental choice of child care.

Family day care clearly has a solid, if diminishing, role in the child care marketplace. Its most loyal customers are mothers of infants and toddlers and mothers who work part-time. Family day care is still a major supplier of out-of-home child care, particularly to infants and toddlers, and tends to be perceived as cheaper than center-based care. Recent cost estimates, however, suggest that family day care and center-based care are similar in price (Hofferth, 1989; Kisker et al., 1989; Sonenstein & Wolf, 1991). Finally, Kahn and Kamerman (1987) point out that the supply of family day care is fairly elastic, able to respond quickly to demand with rapid start-up, little initial investment, and no need for additional buildings or an administrative structure. Thus, to its advocates, family day care is an indispensable component of the child care delivery system in this country that must be nurtured and supported (Emlen, 1973; Sale, 1984, 1986; Adams, 1989). Concerns still exist about the majority of providers who are unregulated and unaccountable to anyone but parents who are not present during the day and who may be unprepared to evaluate the quality of services they are purchasing (Willner, 1969; Enarson, 1991).

Issues and themes: What do we need to know about family day care?

Any policy decisions affecting quality, affordability, and accessibility of child care in this country will undoubtedly involve family day care in some way. It will be crucial to make informed decisions so that expectations are realistic regarding the potential of family day care and its appropriate place in the child care service delivery system. For this very reason, many researchers, policymakers, and policy analysts are aware of the National Day Care Home Study (NDCHS)(Divine-Hawkins, 1981; Fosburg, 1982). This study has been an invaluable resource and has served as a baseline for information on family day care gathered since that time. For all its strengths, however, the NDCHS is limited by the fact that it was conducted only in large urban areas and that the data are now more than a decade old. Although no other study of family day care surpasses the NDCHS in size and scope, compiling the results of more recent studies makes it possible now to go beyond the NDCHS to inform child care policy and practice with more timely research evidence. First it is important to focus on the issues that drive our need for information.

Longevity/turnover. Best estimates indicate that turnover in family day care is as bad as or worse than turnover in center-based care, exceeding 50% annually according to some estimates (NAEYC, 1985). Under these circumstances, continuity of care for children and families is compromised. For family day care to function under optimal conditions, we must better understand what attracts and keeps family day care providers in their jobs. This involves knowledge of the characteristics of providers and their programs as well as their job satisfaction and commitment. In addition, surveying former family day care providers is important in order to understand why caregivers leave their jobs.

Child care as family support. Intuition suggests that family child care has the potential to be more sensitive to individual family needs and thus to be more supportive of families than are center-based programs. For instance, more flexible scheduling; the informal home setting; mixed ages; a single caregiver;

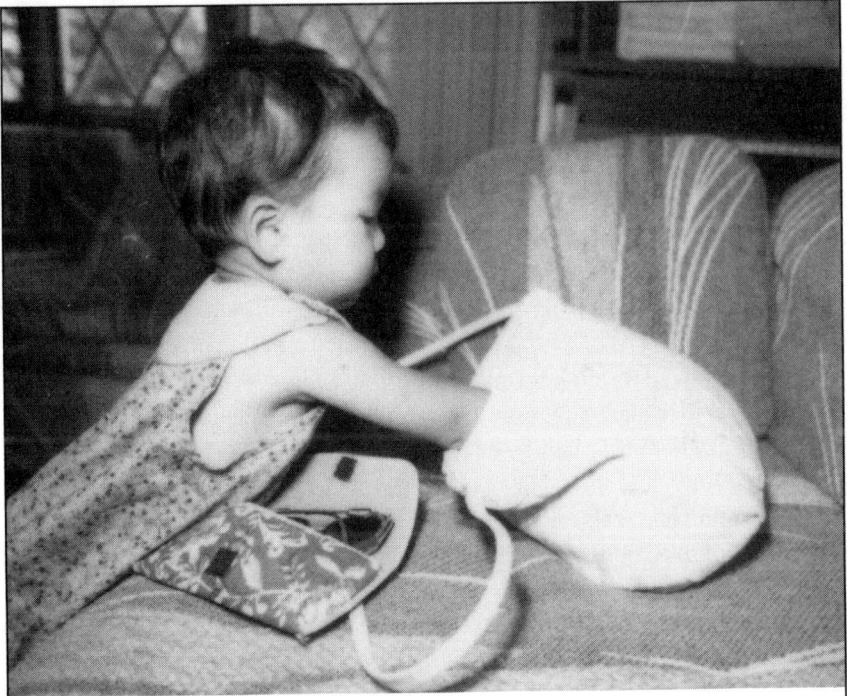

Any policy decisions affecting quality, affordability, and accessibility of child care in this country will undoubtedly involve family day care in some way. It will be crucial to make informed decisions so that expectations are realistic regarding the potential of family day care and its appropriate place in the child care service delivery system.

The purpose of this book is to review the research about family day care so that issues such as turnover, training, and quality can be responded to realistically.

and location in a residential neighborhood differentiate family day care from center-based care, causing many people to view family day care as more closely approximating care by the parent at home and more individualized to family needs. Evidence must be gathered to determine whether our intuitions regarding support to the family by family day care are based on fact.

Regulation. Regulation of family day care varies from state to state (Phillips, Lande, & Goldberg, 1990). Thirty-nine states, the District of Columbia, and the military regulate family day care. Six states regulate only subsidized family day care, three states encourage voluntary registration of family day care homes, and two states do not regulate family day care at all. Questions have been raised about the most effective way to regulate family day care (Class, 1980; Morgan, 1980). Alternative regulatory approaches and how the regulatory climate in each state influences the quality and availability of services are crucial issues for policy and practice.

Training and professionalism. For some, the qualifications for family day care providers should include only those characteristics that are typical of good mothers: love of children, patience, and experience with her own children. This viewpoint implies that training is unnecessary or unlikely to make a difference in the type of care provided because the key qualifications are not typically achieved through formal or informal training; however, research on child care center staff suggests that education and specialized training are important predictors of caregiver effectiveness (Ruopp, Travers, Glantz, & Coelen, 1979; Whitebook, Howes, & Phillips, 1989). We need to investigate how education and training influence family day care providers' knowledge and behavior and, in turn, children's development.

Quality. Family day care has been plagued with an image of custodial care: babies in cribs with propped bottles and preschoolers grouped in front of a television for long hours while a caregiver goes about her business. The NDCHS refuted this stereotype, but the issue of the range and modal level of quality available to families remains. In addition, how the available range of quality predicts children's development is a major concern, with implications for policy and practice.

Compensation and affordability. A survey by NAEYC (1985) revealed that family day care providers typically earn very low wages—some below poverty guidelines. Although low wages may make child care more affordable for families, these wages may also contribute to turnover and lack of job commitment, even among caregivers who love their work with children. Because of these low salaries, family day care providers, like their counterparts in center-based programs, unwittingly subsidize the cost of child care for parents (Culkin, Morris, & Hughes, 1991). This vicious cycle will be broken only if policymakers and parents are adequately informed of the problem and its consequences.

* * *

This monograph will review the family day care knowledge base that is relevant to these key issues. This knowledge base will be divided into six sections (chapters) according to its focus. The first section will examine the ecology of family day care. How caregivers and children behave in family day care, caregiver-child interactions, variations in quality, and the effects of family day care enrollment on children's development will be discussed. The second and third sections will include descriptive data of family day care providers including their personal, professional, and program characteristics. The fourth section will focus on the clientele of family day care. Family and child characteristics, parents' satisfaction with child care, and provider-family relationships will be addressed. In the fifth section, training methods and outcomes will be reviewed. The efficacy of training for family day care providers is of major concern as is the motivation of providers to seek training. The sixth section will examine the regulatory climate in the United States by specifically comparing states with respect to licensing versus registration, how regulatory status is determined, group sizes, training requirements, and age-level limitations. Included in this discussion will be methods of family day care accreditation or credentialing. Each section will be followed by a discussion of the implications of the research on policy and practice. In the final chapter we will revisit the original six key issues and look toward the future. Thus, by the end of the monograph, readers should have a grasp on the knowledge base to inform their opinions on the six key issues influencing the place of family day care in the child care service delivery system.

Chapter 2

The Ecology of Family Day Care

FAMILY DAY CARE IS A UNIQUE CONTEXT IN WHICH TO NURTURE CHILDREN—a context that in certain respects resembles a family environment but in other respects resembles a center environment. Because family day care settings are home-based and serve fewer children than do centers, the link to family environments is logical and inevitable. The number of children served in a regulated family day care home, however, is usually greater than the number of children in a typical American family and, in some states, is closer to the adult-child ratio of a center than of a home. Family day care homes typically group children heterogeneously by age, unlike centers, but because of the number of children, there is a greater likelihood of more than one child being of the same age than in a family. It would usually be biologically impossible for a family to replicate the age mix of family day care homes. Ultimately, we must conclude that family day care differs from both families and centers along enough dimensions to treat it as a separate ecological system (Goelman, 1986). In this chapter, an attempt will be made to characterize this ecological system by examining the research on the "process" of child care in family day care settings. Process refers to what happens in a family day care home, what influences caregivers and children, and why. It is this aspect of child care (center- or home-based) about which we know the least (Long, Peters, & Garduque, 1985). We will analyze what caregivers and children do in family day care, how they behave, and what predicts those behaviors. In addition, developmental outcomes for the children who are being nurtured in family day care environments will be examined. Finally, implications will be drawn for policy and practice as well as for future research. Because family day care is being treated as a separate ecological system from center-based day care, studies whose prime purpose is to compare the similarities and differences of the two settings will not be included in this review.

Activities: What do children and caregivers do?

One of the first studies to present a profile of what happens in family day care was based on the observations of 162 family day care providers in Pennsylvania (Peters, 1972). The profile presented was in some respects a sobering one. The most frequent activity observed was watching television (56 of 162 homes), while the least frequent was story reading (6 of 162 homes). Also relatively frequently observed were informal activities (33 of 162 homes)—presumably unplanned play activities selected by the children to occupy their time. Sociodramatic play, music, and crafts were infrequently observed in these homes (16 or fewer of the 162 homes). One could infer from these data that caregivers were providing a rather sterile, unstimulating environment for the children and were, perhaps, busy with other things. Other data from this study do not totally support this inference, however, because approximately half of the caregivers (80 of 162) spent all of their time with the children during the day and only a few (25 of 162) spent more time on other things away from the children. Verbal contact between caregivers and children was rated as moderate to high for the large majority of homes (125 of 162), and children's involvement in activities was typically rated as moderate to high (129 of 162). The image depicted in the Peters study is one of caregivers involved with children but in the context of informal, child-selected activities. Because of observers' reports that half of the caregivers had few or no play materials for the children, the level of stimulation provided by such informal activities may have been less than optimal in some homes.

A subsequent study conducted in Canada (Johnson, 1981) concluded that family day care homes provide unstimulating care that is not geared to the needs of young children. Based on visits and interviews with 25 caregivers, Johnson estimated that children were spending one-fourth of their total time in care in front of the television (or two hours daily, on the average). One-third of the caregivers had no toys for the children to play with. Book reading and story telling, however, as well as structured games and puzzles, were reported by the majority of caregivers to be daily activities. The least frequent activities reported were gross motor, cooking, and sand play. When the caregivers were placed into a high-, moderate-, or low-quality category based on the variety and frequency of their daily activities for children, 20% of the caregivers were

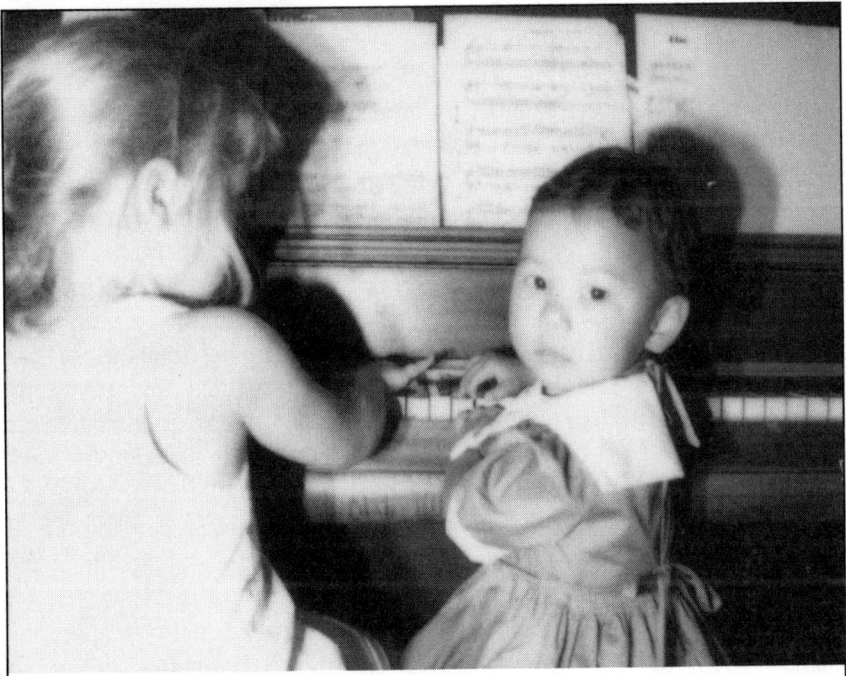

The research on activities in family day care has both positive and negative implications. Several studies suggest that some family day care homes provide unstimulating environments for young children. It is of concern, for instance, that many caregivers are insufficiently supplied with play materials and plan few play activities for children, even resorting to television as an entertainment device or initiating developmentally inappropriate activities. On the other hand, several studies document educational interactions among children and caregivers, high involvement of caregivers with children, and minimal television viewing. Results of these two groups of studies appear to conflict with each other.

Having children of mixed ages for a child to mingle and play with seems to be a plus for family day care homes.

rated high quality and 20% were rated low quality. The remaining 60% of the caregivers were judged to be moderate in quality. In spite of the amount of television viewing in these family day care homes, the majority of caregivers could be characterized as providing moderate- to high-quality care on the basis of the activities they provided. Still, the number of caregivers in this study (as well as in Peters' Pennsylvania study) whose activities were limited by the unavailability of play materials is a concern.

The National Day Care Home Study (NDCHS)(Divine-Hawkins, 1981; Fosburg, 1982), the first national study of family day care, attempted to characterize the daily activities of children and caregivers in family day care through observation. This study revealed that caregivers spent 46% of their time in direct interaction with the children and that this time was spent in appropriate ways. Teaching, helping, and playing/participating were the most frequently observed caregiver interactions with children. Caregivers were uninvolved with children approximately one-third of the time (37%), much of which was occupied by housekeeping. The researchers inferred from these data that these family day care homes were not lacking in stimulation. These conclusions were further reinforced by the finding that children spent only about two percent of their time watching television. Little sociodramatic play and few gross motor, fine motor, or music/dance activities were observed. Caregivers, however, were more heavily involved in stimulating language and in meeting children's physical needs. Overall, the observers were impressed by the quality of care offered by the family day care homes participating in the study (Fosburg, 1982).

There are mixed messages in the research regarding the quality or appropriateness of activities provided by caregivers in family day care. Both Peters and Johnson suggested that less-than-ideal activities were provided in family day care, whereas the NDCHS, with a larger, more geographically diverse sample, was more positive about their data regarding caregiver-and-child activities. Matters are further complicated by other studies attempting to clarify the same terrain.

Wandersman (1978) observed 19 family day care homes and found that caregivers actively participated with the children 25% of the time and observed the children 15% of the time. Little caregiver time was devoted to direct teaching. Wandersman considered the small amount of direct teaching appropriate for the setting and the age of the children. Innes, Woodman,

Banspach, Thompson, and Inwald (1982) observed caregiver-child interaction for 20 children in four large group day care homes. The researchers found that by far the most frequently observed behavior was "positive group contact," defined as "teacher-initiated behavior directed toward the group," involving such activities as "storytelling, lesson plans, and skits." These results appear to be counter to those of Wandersman, perhaps because they are based on a very small sample of large family day care homes. Consistent with other studies (Peters, 1972; Fosburg, 1982), however, children were rarely observed in sociodramatic play (2%; Innes et al., 1982).

Several more recent studies have provided glimpses into the types of activities offered by family day care providers. According to Aguirre (1987), for instance, the vast majority of caregivers in his sample reported reading stories (98%), providing art activities (coloring, drawing, painting; 92%), working on the alphabet or "letter readiness" (83%), and doing "nature" activities (76%). The least frequently reported activities were dancing (34%) and dramatic play (22%). Self-report data of this type must be interpreted with some caution because one never knows to what extent it could be confirmed through observation.

Rosenthal (1988) observed 41 Israeli family day care providers as they went about their normal daily activities. She found that "educational activities" initiated by the caregiver accounted for 26% of the children's time in care, and that children spent 23% of their time in group interaction with the caregiver. Thus, nearly half of the children's time was spent in some sort of interaction with peers and/or the caregiver.

A less positive portrayal of life in family day care was provided by Eheart and Leavitt (1989) through interviews and in-depth observations of six caregivers over a 10-month period. Most of the caregivers indicated that they allowed the children to play freely for most of the day without structure being imposed. Four of the six caregivers had insufficient amounts of play materials for the children (one caregiver required children to bring their own play materials), and, not surprisingly, children were observed to be frustrated and bored. Five of the six caregivers rarely planned for or extended children's play. All six caregivers tried to initiate play activities with the children but reported being frequently dissatisfied with the results. It appeared that their lack of success was sometimes due to inappropriate selection of activities (e.g., "Simon Says" for preschoolers and toddlers). One caregiver said she was allowing more television watching than she liked because of her inability to keep the children entertained in any other way. The researchers inferred from their observations and conversations with family day care providers that the daily experiences of young children in family day care homes may not always be as positive as reported in the NDCHS.

Summary

The research on activities in family day care has both positive and negative implications. Several studies suggest that some family day care homes provide unstimulating environments for young children. It is of concern, for instance, that many caregivers are insufficiently supplied with play materials and plan few play activities for children, even resorting to television as an entertainment device or initiating developmentally inappropriate activities. On the other hand, several studies documented educational interactions among children and caregivers, high involvement of caregivers with children, and minimal television viewing. Results of these two groups of studies appear to conflict with each other.

To resolve this conflict, it is informative to consider the methods used to gather data in each of the studies. Those studies that conducted actual "behavior counts" of children and caregivers (Wandersman, 1978; Divine-Hawkins, 1981; Innes et al., 1982; Rosenthal, 1988) reported the most positive results. The studies based on more informal ratings, observations, and interviews (Peters, 1972; Johnson, 1981; Eheart & Leavitt, 1989) resulted in more negative portrayals of family day care homes. It is impossible to say that one method is more valid than the other, assuming they are both carried out soundly. We could, however, infer that to accurately depict activities in family day care requires multiple research methods using both qualitative and quantitative approaches. Future studies must include both approaches in order to accurately determine the nature and appropriateness of the activities provided in family day care in which caregivers and children engage. Based on existing research we must presume that—consistent with other forms of child care—although many family day care homes provide stimulating environments for their charges, many others are deficient in the materials and activities available and thus are less-than-ideal places for children.

How are caregiver behaviors related to caregiver characteristics and conditions of caregiving?

Surprisingly few studies have addressed this question. There appears to be more interest in the outcome of caregiver behavior as seen through children's behavior and development (see next section). In spite of their unequal treatment in the research, these issues are equally important for explaining the ecology of family day care, as demonstrated by Long, Peters, and Garduque (1985) in their proposed model of family and child care influences on children's development. Caregiver characteristics and conditions of caregiving are both hypothesized to predict caregiver behavior that, in turn, influences child behavior. The model suggests that conditions of caregiving directly affect children's development but also indirectly affect it through caregiver behaviors. Caregiver characteristics, on the other hand, are shown solely as indirect influences on children's development, being mediated by caregiver behavior. In other words, the relationship of caregiver behavior to children's development cannot be fully understood without an explanation of how caregiver characteristics and conditions of caregiving determine that behavior.

Caregiver characteristics

Several studies have examined the association between caregiver training and caregiver behavior. These studies will be reviewed in Chapter 6. Training has consistently been found to have a positive association with caregiver behavior or the quality of care provided. In contrast, few significant relationships have been found between caregivers' behavior and their years of education or experience; neither Divine-Hawkins (1981) nor Rosenthal (1990) found such relationships in their respective studies. Howes (1983), on the other hand, found that family day care providers with more experience in child care expressed less negative affect, were less restrictive, and were more likely to respond positively to toddler social bids. There may be insufficient variability in caregivers' educational levels to yield significant relationships with other variables. The impact of experience on caregiver behavior needs further examination.

The NDCHS (Divine-Hawkins, 1981; Stallings, 1981) also examined the impact of ethnicity and geographic location on caregiver behavior. When caregiver age, education, experience, and regulatory status were controlled, few differences in caregiver behavior could be attributed to ethnicity. Black caregivers tended to be more directive than were White or Hispanic caregivers, and White caregivers interacted less frequently with school-age children than

The number of children in care and caregiver training may be particularly important variables associated with caregiver behavior. Results of research support group-size restrictions in family day care regulations as well as restrictions on the number of infants and toddlers allowed in a group. From a regulatory perspective, using training as an indicator of family day care providers' qualifications appears to have more support than using education or experience. Variables that seem particularly important to study in the future include the amount of supervision of caregivers, caregivers' years of experience, and the extensiveness of child-designed space.

did Hispanic and Black caregivers. According to Stallings, these differences were so few that they could have occurred by chance and thus should not be interpreted as conclusive.

There were some significant geographic location differences among the NDCHS caregivers after controlling for education and ethnicity. According to Stallings, caregivers in Philadelphia tended to spend more time teaching and interacting with the children than did caregivers in other areas of the country. They also promoted more language/information and involvement with housework and expressed more negative affect than did caregivers at other sites. Caregivers in San Antonio were more directive and controlling. They more often promoted gross motor activities and prosocial behavior than did caregivers at other sites. Stallings suggested that these differences could be attributed to differences in climate and housing, pace of living, and the regulatory context; no policy implications were drawn, however.

Conditions of caregiving

Number of children. The NDCHS (Divine-Hawkins, 1981) found that the frequency of caregivers' interactions with individual children decreased as the group size increased, but that interactions with groups of two or more children increased. Howes' (1983) study of 20 toddlers in family day care showed that caregivers caring for more children talked less, expressed more negative affect, were more restrictive, were more likely to ignore a request, and were less likely to respond positively to a toddler's social bid. Consistent with these findings, Stith and Davis (1984) found that the greater the number of children, the fewer positive caregiver behaviors (e.g., expression of positive affect, contingent responses to stress) were observed in a very small sample of family day care providers (10). The results of these three studies suggest that larger group sizes with a single caregiver have a detrimental effect on caregiver behavior in family day care.

Age of children. The NDCHS (Divine-Hawkins, 1981; Stallings, 1981) revealed differences in caregiver behavior as a function of the age mix of the children. Caregivers did less teaching, playing, and watching television with the older children when infants were present. In homes with toddlers, caregivers

It appears that many family day care homes do not encourage pretend play. Some even lack an assortment of basic toys. Reading stories is a common activity.

were more directive and less likely to provide messy materials (such as paint, play dough, and so forth). When there were more preschool children, caregivers did more language stimulation. The greater the age mix, the less the caregiver talked to the younger children.

Wandersman (1981) found that caregivers caring for more younger children reported more role strain and emotional drain from caregiving than caregivers with more older preschool children. Infants and toddlers appear to be more demanding on caregivers, making it more difficult for them to behave in optimal ways. A study conducted in Israel partially confirms these results (Rosenthal, 1990). Caregivers whose average child's age was greater provided a higher quality environment than those caring for younger children. Older children were provided better physical care conditions, more varied toys, a better organized and less crowded space, and more planned educational activities. The quality of interaction between caregiver and child, however, did not vary as a function of the average age of the children. Thus, although there is some evidence that the age of the children has an impact on caregiver behavior, more research is needed to determine how robust this relationship is.

Other factors. Other aspects of the conditions of caregiving in family child care have been investigated in only one study, rendering any conclusions tentative. Howes (1983) looked at how the number of hours per day of contact with children, the amount of housework done during the day, and the extensiveness of child-designed space were associated with caregiver behavior. Contact hours per day and amount of housework were associated with ignoring toddlers' requests. Caregivers who worked in more child-designed space were more likely to express positive affect and less likely to express negative affect or to restrict toddler activity. Rosenthal (1990) included intensity of caregiver supervision and proportion of "problem" families as conditions of caregiving. Results revealed that caregivers receiving at least weekly supervision provided higher quality interactions, and caregivers with more problem families provided lower quality interactions. Of these five additional factors, the intensity of caregiver supervision and the amount of child-designed space appeared to have the most potent effect on caregiver behavior and deserve more attention in future research.

Summary

Caregiver characteristics and conditions of caregiving have been shown to relate to caregiver behavior. The number of children in care and caregiver training may be particularly important variables associated with caregiver behavior. Results of research support group-size restrictions in family day care regulations as well as restrictions on the number of infants and toddlers allowed in a group. From a regulatory perspective, using training as an indicator of family day care providers' qualifications appears to have more support than using education or experience. Variables that seem particularly important to study in the future include the amount of supervision of caregivers, caregivers' years of experience, and the extensiveness of child-designed space.

Relationship of caregiver characteristics and behavior and conditions of caregiving to children's behavior and development

Caregiver characteristics

It is reasonable to think that children in family day care may be influenced by the background their caregivers bring to their work. Few studies have investigated the relationship of caregiver characteristics to children's behavior and development; in those that have, the findings are mixed. Clarke-Stewart (1986; 1987) found no relationship between children's cognitive or social competence and caregiver training (few of the caregivers had any type of training). Education and knowledge of child development, however, were each correlated with one aspect of social competence.

In a study of Swedish children in family day care (Lamb, Sternberg, & Knuth, 1989), there were associations between caregivers' education and caregiver (but not parent) ratings of children's personality maturity but none with quality of children's peer play. Caregivers' training negatively predicted both positive and negative peer play. In other words, children in family day

Our knowledge of the ecology of family day care is still in its infancy.

care homes with more trained caregivers exhibited both less positive and less negative peer play.

Kontos (1990) reported significant correlations between caregiver experience and children's cognitive development as well as between caregiver specialized training in child care and ratings of children's social development. In addition, more nurturing childrearing attitudes on the part of caregivers were associated with more language interaction and higher levels of peer play but lower ratings of social development for the children. Caregiver education was not related to any aspect of children's behavior or development.

Caregiver behavior

The first study to examine the relationship between caregiver behavior and children's development in family child care was the New York Infant Day Care Study (Golden, Rosenbluth, Grossi, Policare, Freeman, & Brownlee, 1979). This was a longitudinal study following the development of nearly 400 children from their enrollment in center-based or family day care as infants until they were age three. Children's cognitive, language, social, and emotional functioning were assessed at approximately six-month intervals. Caregivers' individual attention to as well as cognitive, language, social, and emotional stimulation of the children were observed. Unfortunately, the correlational analysis for caregiver behaviors and children's development combined caregivers and children in center-based and family day care, making it impossible to attribute any associations between variables to conditions in either centers or family day care homes. Results of the analysis revealed that cognitive-language and socioemotional stimulation by caregivers at 24 months correlated significantly with children's language competence and social competence with adults at age three. Also, caregivers' socioemotional stimulation of children at 24 months predicted children's adequacy of emotional functioning at age three. Thus, this study led the way in suggesting that, regardless of the child care setting, caregiver behaviors are related to children's development.

More recently, Clarke-Stewart (Clarke-Stewart & Gruber, 1984; Clarke-Stewart, 1986, 1987) conducted a study of 130 children in one of four forms of care: home with mother, home with sitter, day care home, or day care center.

Few studies have simultaneously assessed caregiver characteristics, conditions of caregiving, caregiver behavior, and overall child care quality in addition to process and outcome measures of children's development and family background factors.

The family day care group consisted of 20 children whose average age was approximately 32 months. A variety of measures of caregiver behaviors and children's development were obtained. Assessments were made of caregivers' individual and group social, verbal, and physical interactions with children; affection; helping and playing with children; teaching; reading; directiveness; control; responsiveness; verbal demands; and so forth. Regarding children, assessments were made of their cognitive ability, social knowledge, sociability to a stranger in the lab and in the home, proximity to mother, reciprocity to mother, positive/negative initiations to peers, and social competence at home.

For the purposes of the analysis, the family day care group was combined with the in-home babysitter group, thus obscuring interpretations regarding family day care. Significant correlations between caregiver behaviors and children's development were relatively numerous but small to moderate in size (range = .19 to .37). Only some of the more substantial correlations will be mentioned here. Children's cognitive abilities were positively associated with caregiver responsiveness and with the caregiver reading to them and negatively associated with caregiver help-giving and directiveness. Children's reciprocity with their mothers was positively associated with caregiver responsiveness. Social knowledge was negatively associated with caregiver help-giving. Clarke-Stewart (1986) summarized the associations this way: ". . . children from day-care homes in our study did better in the assessments of intellectual and social competence when the caregiver had more one-to-one conversations with them and when she touched, read to and gave more directions to them. . . . Children in day care homes also were more intellectually advanced when the quality of the caregiver's behavior toward them was more responsive. Moreover, children whose caregivers were more positive, demanding, and responsive were observed to have more positive, reciprocal, and cooperative interactions with their mothers in our laboratory assessment. Children whose caregivers were less didactic and controlling exhibited the immature pattern of staying physically closer to their mothers in our laboratory observation" (p. 43).

Rothstein-Fisch and Howes (1988) observed the peer play of 30 toddlers in family day care homes. Their results revealed that caregiver activity (interacting with children or participating in day care-related tasks, such as housework, leisure, interviewing a new parent) was related to complexity of peer play. The

For now, knowing that the relationships exist among these various factors should be sufficient incentive to promote practices that we think can optimize the developmental potential of family day care.

toddlers in this study engaged in more complex play when the caregiver was not interacting with them.

Although the results of Rothstein-Fisch and Howes may seem counterintuitive, another study of 57 children in 30 different family day care homes (Dunn & Kontos, 1989; Kontos, 1990) obtained similar results. In this study, the complexity of children's peer play was negatively correlated with the frequency of caregivers' high-level involvement (touching, smiling, and talking) with them and positively correlated with the frequency of caregivers' low-level involvement (routine caregiving with little or no affect or talking). The results of these two studies suggest that caregivers' involvement in children's peer play does not necessarily facilitate its complexity. On the other hand, Kontos (1990) found positive associations between caregivers' average level of involvement and frequency of high levels of involvement with the children and children's language in the family day care home. Thus, although caregivers' interactions may not facilitate peer play, they may facilitate other aspects of development, such as language.

Rosenthal's (1990) study of Israeli family day care provides additional evidence regarding the relationship between caregiver behavior and children's development. Children in family day care homes in which caregivers engaged in higher quality interactions were more competent and did less aimless wandering. They were less likely to play alone or near another child and spent more time in group activities. Quality of caregiver interaction made no difference to children's gross motor behavior, concept and skill acquisition, or emotional distress.

Conditions of caregiving

The New York Infant Day Care Study (Golden, Rosenbluth, Grossi, Policare, Brownlee, & Freeman, 1979) examined conditions of caregiving in the same way it did caregiver behavior, grouping together the results for centers and family day care homes. A physical stimulation index that indicated the availability and variety of play materials and equipment, adequacy of play space, toilet facilities, ventilation, lighting, and cleanliness was determined for each child care setting. Adult-child ratio was also calculated. Neither variable was correlated with any measure of children's development.

This awareness should also encourage research that more clearly informs us of what optimal family day care should be.

In Wandersman's (1981) study, children in family day care homes with greater numbers of children engaged in more highly intellectual activities, more interaction with peers, and fewer negative socioemotional expressions. In other words, group size was associated with positive outcomes. Another view is provided by Howes and Rubenstein (1985), who found that there were more incidents of "restrict and cry" between caregivers and toddlers in family day care homes with larger groups. Adult-child ratio was negatively associated with "talk and play" between caregivers and toddlers. Kontos (1990) found no correlations between group size and children's development. A study of family day care in Utah with a very small sample (n = 18; Lamb, Sternberg, & Knuth, 1989) also found no significant correlations between group size and either quality of children's peer play or children's personality development.

Clarke-Stewart (1986) reported in her study that when group size was moderate (two to five), children in family day care homes exhibited more social knowledge and were more socially competent (it is not clear in her report how she came to these conclusions, however). Interestingly, in family day care homes with more dangerous and messy environments, the children were less socially competent in their own homes.

Summary

Making sense of these data is hindered by the small number of studies and complicated by the fact that the family day care and child outcome variables have been measured differently in each study. It appears that caregiver behavior contributes both positively and negatively to child outcomes in family day care and that these associations warrant further investigation. Results on conditions of caregiving are mixed. The most frequently used measure is group size or adult-child ratio (these measures are the same in family day care homes with one caregiver). Results of research on the effects of group size and adult-child ratio on children in family day care are equivocal, suggesting that further research is warranted. It is important to note that, in spite of the numerous associations of child outcomes with caregiver characteristics, behaviors, and conditions of caregiving, these associations are frequently small and present for a minority of the child outcome measures. The field has far to go in its understanding of the relationships among these variables.

Relationship of family day care quality to children's behavior and development

Although several studies have examined quality in family day care as a function of regulatable features such as group size and adult-child ratio (e.g. Howes & Rubenstein, 1985), the studies to be reviewed here have used process-oriented features of the family day care setting to define quality. Three studies have used the Family Day Care Rating Scale (FDCRS) or an adaptation

Children in family day care homes where caregivers engage in high-quality interactions are more competent intellectually and socially. Children in high-quality family day care homes spend less time aimlessly wandering and more time engaged in stimulating activities and interactions.

of it (Harms & Clifford, 1989) and the fourth used the Belsky and Walker (1980) checklist.

Howes and Stewart (1987) studied 55 11- to 30-month-old children in fulltime family day care. The researchers created a weighted composite measure of family day care quality by factor-analyzing the subscale scores of the FDCRS for each family day care home along with group size, number of adults, and adult-child ratio. Because family day care quality was expected to co-vary with family characteristics, measures of family characteristics were factor analyzed to yield two weighted composite measures: (1) nurturing and supported, and (2) restrictive and stressed. Child outcomes measured were level of play with peers, with objects, and with adults. In addition, the child's age of entry into day care and the number of changes in caregiving arrangements were recorded.

Howes and Stewart reported quality-child outcome correlations separately for boys and girls, controlling for age and family characteristics. These data revealed that for both boys and girls, family day care quality was associated with the level of play with objects and adults. For girls only, family day care quality was also associated with the level of play with peers.

Lamb and colleagues (Lamb, Hwang, Bookstein, Broberg, Hult, & Frodi, 1988a; Lamb, Hwang, Broberg, & Bookstein, 1988b) conducted a longitudinal study in Sweden on the development of children's social competence in center-based and family day care as well as in-home care. Family characteristics, quality of home and alternative care, and social support, among other variables, were included in the analysis. Quality of home and alternative care were assessed using the Belsky and Walker (1980) checklist, which consists of 13 positive events (e.g., caregiver positive regard, caregiver verbal elaboration) and 7 negative events (e.g., child crying, caregiver prohibiting child action) that an observer checks for occurrence following a three minute "spot" sample unit. Three to four samples per observation were obtained. Lamb et al. (1988a) found that neither type of care nor quality of alternative care were significant predictors of children's social competence one year after enrollment. Two years after enrollment, however, quality of alternative care was a significant predictor of children's social competence (Lamb et al., 1988b). Unfortunately, these results were not reported separately for center-based and family day care so that, once again, we are unable to attribute results to the effects of family day care.

A study of 18 children (average age = 29 months) in family day care in Salt Lake City, conducted by Lamb, Sternberg, and Knuth (1989), used measures similar to the measures used in the Swedish study (Lamb et al., 1988a; 1988b). Of fourteen correlations computed between the Belsky and Walker (1980) positive and negative scores and the seven child outcome measures (peer play and personality), only one was significant: Higher positive scores were associated with more positive peer play. One significant correlation in fourteen is only slightly different from what one might expect due to chance. Thus, the research by Lamb and his colleagues suggests that quality in family day care is not an important predictor of children's social development. These results are inconsistent with Howes and Stewart's (1987) results, but this discrepancy may be due to the extremely small size of Lamb, Sternberg, and Knuth's sample.

Using the FDCRS (Harms & Clifford, 1989) as the measure of family day care quality in 30 family day care homes (57 children between 30 and 48 months of age), Dunn and Kontos (1989) reported no significant correlations between quality and level of peer or object play. The only significant zero-order correlation between quality and child outcome was for children's receptive language, as measured by the Peabody Picture Vocabulary Test. More recently, a multivariate approach was used to determine the best predictors of children's cognitive, language, and social development among family and caregiver characteristics, family day care quality, and interactions between these aspects (Kontos, 1990). Quality alone, as measured by the FDCRS, was not a significant predictor of any aspect of children's development. The interaction between family day care quality and father's educational level, however, was a significant predictor of both receptive language and cognitive competence (contributing 32% and 38% of the variance, respectively). Family characteristics as mediators of quality influences on children's development will be addressed in the following section.

Rosenthal (1990) adapted the FDCRS (Harms & Clifford, 1989) and the Day Care Environment Inventory (Prescott, Kritchevsky, & Jones, 1972) for Israeli family day care settings caring for infants and toddlers (sample size = 82). In addition, a daily log was kept that continuously recorded the activities of the group and the duration of these activities. A composite measure of the quality of the family day care environment was derived from these three measures. The measure consisted of standard scores for physical care conditions, amount and variety of play materials, organization of play materials, crowdedness, daily schedule, proportion of educational and physical care group activities, relaxed and pleasant emotional tone, and atmosphere. The findings revealed that children in higher quality family day care environments spent more time in concept and skill acquisition behavior and less time in gross motor activity and aimless wandering. They also spent less time in group activities and more time alone or near another child.

The results regarding associations between quality of family day care and children's development are mixed. This is not surprising given the differences in sample size, geography, ages of children, and types of measures. The nature of family day care in Los Angeles (Howes & Stewart, 1987), central Indiana (Dunn & Kontos, 1989; Kontos, 1990), Utah (Lamb, Sternberg, & Knuth, 1989), and Israel (Rosenthal, 1990) is likely to be quite different. When these differences are complicated by assessing children of different ages regarding different aspects of development, it is no wonder the results lack congruence. Nonetheless, taken together, the research suggests that further exploration of the contribution of family day care quality to children's development is warranted. Certain aspects of quality may well be important for certain aspects of children's development at certain ages. Research designs must be employed that can tease out these differential effects and thus be more informative regarding the effects of family day care quality on children.

Family factors as moderators of family day care quality influences on children

To say that children are not randomly assigned to child care environments is perhaps stating the obvious. Families must select for their children from child care options available to them. Thus, family day care influences on children are logically linked to the family characteristics that led to or are associated with its selection. Several studies have attempted to confirm this linkage empirically.

Clarke-Stewart (Clarke-Stewart, 1984; Clarke-Stewart & Gruber, 1984) included both family and child measures in her study of "day care forms and features." In one analysis of these data (Clarke-Stewart & Gruber, 1984), significant correlations between physical characteristics of the family day care setting and children's cognitive development disappeared when family socioeconomic status was statistically controlled. Clarke-Stewart and Gruber suggested that this phenomenon may be partially attributable to patterns of parental selection of particular family day care environments. In another analysis of these data, comparisons of families using different forms of child care revealed that parents using family day care had lower socioeconomic status than parents using center-based care (Clarke-Stewart, 1984). Thus, socioeconomic status appeared to be a family variable mediating the effects of family day care quality.

Family characteristics were found to vary with family day care quality in another study (Howes & Stewart, 1987). More nurturing and supportive families were using better quality care, while more restrictive and stressed families were using poorer quality care. Both family characteristics and family day care quality were correlated with the level of children's play behaviors when the other was controlled statistically. These results were interpreted as evidence for an "additive effect" of family and child care influences on children's play in child care.

Rosenthal (1990) included both parental education and quality of the family child care environment (in addition to child's age and quality of interaction) as predictors of children's development. Environmental quality predicted several measures of children's development over and above the effects of parental education. The data revealed, however, that children with more educated parents spent more time in aimless wandering and less time in gross motor activity. Rosenthal suggested that these counterintuitive results may indicate that the family day care environment was not stimulating enough for children of more educated parents.

Another study included both family background and family day care quality variables (Kontos, 1990). One purpose of that study was to determine how both family and child care factors would best predict children's development in family day care. There were no significant relationships between family background and family day care quality. Family background measures generally were better predictors of children's development than family day care quality or other characteristics of the family day care environment (based on number and size of significant correlations). Using a multivariate approach, two family variables—satisfaction with parenting and stress—were the best predictors of ratings of children's intellectual functioning and sociability, respectively. For two other variables, IQ and receptive vocabulary, the interaction of the father's education with family day care quality was the best predictor. In four of the seven child outcome measures, the best models for predicting children's development included a combination of family and child care factors. Although these data did not replicate the "confounding" of family factors and quality found by Howes and Stewart (1987) and inferred by Clarke-Stewart and Gruber (1983), they did confirm the importance of examining both aspects in explaining the development of children in family day care.

Although the number of studies is limited, family background consistently emerges as an important factor to consider when evaluating the effects of family day care on children. Demographic variables as well as stress and childrearing attitudes have been shown to be important family factors to take into account.

Summary and implications

Our knowledge of the ecology of family day care is still in its infancy (Squibb, 1986). Studies are needed that investigate relationships between multiple ecological levels involving children, families, and family day care settings. Few studies have simultaneously assessed caregiver characteristics, conditions of caregiving, caregiver behavior, and overall child care quality in addition to process and outcome measures of children's development and family background factors. Inclusion of so many variables requires large samples. Moreover, given regional differences in child care regulations, the child care marketplace, and demographic characteristics of families, multisite samples would be desirable in order to increase the validity and generalizability of results. Needless to say, an effort of this type would be expensive and labor-intensive but necessary to answer complicated questions regarding the ecology of family day care.

In spite of the tentative nature of this body of research, there is sufficient evidence to confirm that caregiver characteristics and conditions of caregiving *do* influence caregivers, who, in turn, influence children. In other words, who their caregivers are and what these caregivers do with their young charges makes a difference to children developmentally. What we have yet to pin down is exactly what the relationships among these factors are, particularly regarding associations with child outcomes. On one hand, fairly consistent evidence is building regarding the negative relationships of group size and number of infants and toddlers, and the positive relationship of training, with caregiver behavior. On the other hand, we have evidence that caregiver behavior is related to children's behavior, but the research cannot tell us under what conditions these associations are positive versus negative and for which developmental outcomes. Drawing implications for policy and practice under such circumstances is difficult and risky. For now, knowing that the relationships exist among these various factors should be sufficient incentive to promote practices that we think can optimize the developmental potential of family day care and also to encourage research that more clearly informs us of what optimal family day care should be.

Chapter 3

Characteristics of Caregivers: Who Are They?

WATTENBERG (1980) REFERRED TO FAMILY DAY CARE AS "the last of the cottage industries." Family day care providers may form the largest single group of home-based workers in our economy (Nelson, 1988). Family day care is unique in that it transforms a woman's traditional caregiving role into self-employment. Who chooses this form of work, and why? To gain insight into how family day care functions in this country, it is necessary to understand who the caregivers are. The purpose of this chapter is to examine the characteristics of family day care providers. Demographic and work-related characteristics of caregivers will be described. Implications of caregiver characteristics for family day care service delivery will be discussed. A number of studies have looked into the question, *Who are the caregivers?*

National Day Care Home Study

The first systematic effort to answer this question was the National Day Care Home Study (NDCHS) (Divine-Hawkins, 1981; Fosburg, 1982). The NDCHS was the first national study of family day care and the first attempt to characterize, among other things, the women who provide family day care; family child care providers are almost always women. The study was conducted in three urban settings—Los Angeles, Philadelphia, and San Antonio—between 1976 and 1980. The sample was selected to represent the typical ethnicity of caregivers and the form of their family day care home (based on regulatory status and administrative structure) in urban settings. A core sample of 793 caregivers who were White, Black, or Hispanic and either unregulated, regulated, or sponsored (member of a day care system under the sponsorship of an umbrella agency) was identified. In addition, 2,812 children cared for in these caregivers' homes were included in the study. An in-depth study was conducted of 303 of the core sample of caregivers and the children in their care. Both interviews of adults (caregivers and parents) and observations of adults and children were obtained.

These data revealed that, on the average, caregivers were 41.6 years of age and cared for 3.5 children other than their own. Seventy-six percent of the caregivers had a high school diploma or less (19% had an 8th grade education or less), and 50% had one to seven years of experience in family day care (25% had less than one year of experience). Exposure to training varied with the form of family day care. Nearly three-fourths of caregivers in sponsored homes had received some training, while caregivers in less than one-third of regulated homes and approximately one-fifth of the unregulated homes had received any training. The vast majority of caregivers had children of their own and were thus experienced in caring for children. On the other hand, hardly any caregivers had any previous experience with children outside the home (e.g., in nursery schools or day care centers). The caregivers were typically married (75%), so they were not providing the sole family income. Median family income was $10,000 (not updated for inflation). Caregivers liked their work, most frequently said they were involved in family day care because they loved children, and considered their work a permanent job. A profile of the typical family day care provider begins to emerge from these data.

What this description of the typical caregiver in the NDCHS fails to portray, however, is the diversity found among the caregivers. For instance, the age range of caregivers was 16 to 76 years old. Ethnicity was related to differences in *years of education* (50% of Hispanic caregivers never went past grade school, but only 5% of White and 10% of Black caregivers did); *age* (White caregivers were more likely to be younger than the average and to have preschool children of their own at home); and *marital status* (80% of White and Hispanic caregivers were married, but only 50% of Black caregivers). A substantial portion of the caregivers (25%) had considerable experience, ranging from 7 to 36 years. Clearly, a profile of typical family day care provider characteristics masks the group's diversity. It is important to keep in mind both what is typical and the diversity that characterizes family day care providers.

Studies of family day care before and since the NDCHS have rarely included a sample of caregivers as diverse as the NDCHS did. In particular, inclusion of variety in the ethnicity of caregivers and the regulatory status of family day care homes in the samples studied has been atypical. In spite of that fact, the results of studies characterizing family day care providers are remarkably consistent with those of the NDCHS.

Family day care is unique in that it transforms a woman's traditional caregiving role into self-employment. Who chooses this form of work, why, and what kinds of services do they offer?

Personal characteristics

Age

Studies that have included the caregiver's age as a variable have nearly uniformly found the average to be between 34 and 37 years of age, a bit younger than reported in the NDCHS (Emlen, Donoghue, & LaForge, 1971; Bryant et al., 1980; Eheart & Leavitt, 1986; Cox & Richarz, 1987; Pence & Goelman, 1987b; Rosenthal, 1988; Bollin, 1989; Fischer, 1989; Goelman et al., 1990). Kisker et al. (1989) reported average ages between 39 and 44, but these numbers were inflated by including the ages of relatives, many of whom were grandparents, caring for children. According to the National Association for the Education of Young Children (NAEYC) (1985), 50% of family day care providers are older than 35. Two studies that reported the average ages of Black family day care providers found that, consistent with the NDCHS, they were older than the White caregivers (Rose, 1976; Eheart & Leavitt, 1986). Thus, it may be accurate to portray the typical White family day care provider as in her midthirties and the typical Black or Hispanic caregiver as in her midforties, keeping in mind the large variability.

Marital status

There is one characteristic of family day care providers that is consistent across studies: The majority are married. NAEYC (1985) and the NDCHS (Divine-Hawkins, 1981; Fosburg, 1982) reported that 25% of caregivers in family day care were single wage earners—figures consistent with Kontos (1989) and Gramley (1990). Other studies have found the proportion of married caregivers to be even higher, ranging from 80% to 98% (Emlen et al., 1971; Bryant et al., 1980; Cox & Richarz, 1987; Kontos, 1988a; Rosenthal, 1988; Bollin, 1990). Thus, it is possible to say unequivocally that most family day care providers are married. It is important to remember, however, that few of these samples were ethnically diverse, an important distinction in light of the finding by the NDCHS (Fosburg, 1982) that significantly more Black than White caregivers were single. The fact that a majority of family day care providers is married is probably because their typical earnings are insufficient for supporting a family (see section on income, forthcoming).

A profile of the "typical" family day care provider's characteristics masks the diversity of the group. However, the results of studies characterizing family day care providers are remarkably consistent.

Family size

Several studies have reported the number of children in the caregivers' own families. In addition to knowing the total number of children, an important distinction is the number of children receiving care versus the number in school all day or out of the home. The data reported do not always allow this distinction to be made.

In general, the data indicate that family day care providers typically have one to three children of their own, and a significant proportion of those children are age six or older and thus are not cared for during the day. This is not a very precise estimate, but reflects the variation in the results of research. Reports on the average total number of children have varied from 1.2 to 3.5 (Emlen et al., 1971; Emlen, Donaghue, & Clarkson, 1974; Cox & Richarz, 1987; Kontos, 1988a; Rosenthal, 1988; Bollin, 1989). Frequently, caregivers' children are school age or older. In one sample 38% of the caregivers had school-age children (Emlen et al., 1971), and in another sample 80% had children school age or older (Rosenthal, 1988). The majority of caregivers' children in another study were school age or older, but unlicensed caregivers were more likely than were licensed caregivers to have children age five or younger (Fischer, 1989). Similarly, Cox and Richarz (1987) found that the typical family day care provider in their sample had more than two children, and the children's average age was more than nine years.

Education

Education, training, and experience in family day care are three related factors likely to have an impact on caregiver behavior. Consistent with the NDCHS, most research has shown that the typical family day care provider has a high school diploma or less (Emlen et al., 1971; Bryant et al., 1980; NAEYC, 1985; Abbot-Shim & Kaufman, 1986; Eheart & Leavitt, 1986; Moss, 1987; Kontos, 1988a; Rosenthal, 1988; Fisher, 1989). In several studies, however, average educational attainment was a year or two beyond high school, or the figures included significant proportions of caregivers who had one or two years of postsecondary education (Abbot-Shim & Kaufman, 1986; Cox & Richarz, 1987; Bollin, 1989; Kontos, 1989; Jones, 1991). NAEYC (1985) reported that, whereas the average educational attainment for family day care providers was 11.3 years, or slightly less than a high school diploma, 30% had some postsecondary education. Very few family day care providers have college degrees, with reports varying from 12% (Eheart & Leavitt, 1986) to 3.5% (Fisher, 1989). In general, the research suggests that a high school diploma is the typical educational level of family day care providers.

Income

There is little information available regarding the income of family day care providers. What little is known is reported in various ways, including total household income, income from family day care, and hourly/weekly rates per child (the latter will be reported in Chapter 4). Another complicating factor is that these data quickly become difficult to compare and interpret due to inflation. Thus, these data will be reported in order to provide a general idea of the income of family day care providers.

As one might expect, studies do document increases in average household income over time. For instance, Emlen et al. (1971) reported the average annual household income for caregivers in Portland, Oregon, in the late 1960s to be approximately $7,000. In the late 1970s, the caregivers participating in the NDCHS reported a median annual household income of $10,000. Two recent studies conducted in the late 1980s reported the average caregiver's annual household income to be approximately $30,000 (Fischer, 1989; Bollin, 1990). On the other hand, Cox and Richarz (1987) reported that the median family income was $17,500 for regulated family child care providers and $20,714 for unregulated caregivers.

It is wrong to conclude from these data that the expendable household income of family day care providers has nearly doubled or tripled in the last 10 years, as appears to be the case. The most obvious influence on income has been inflation. Another factor is location. In a three-site study of child care in urban areas, family incomes of family day care providers varied considerably by site (Kisker et al., 1989). For instance, in Newark, 42% of the caregivers' families earned $12,000 or less, whereas in South Chicago, family income for 39% of the caregivers was $24,000 or more. Regardless of location, however, the least frequent income categories were those between $12,000 and $24,000 per year (lower-income women may have fewer employment opportunities; higher-income women may be able to "afford" the relatively low earnings typical of family day care). Still another factor may be that the family economic profile of women entering the field of family day care in the 1980s was different than for those in the 1970s, so that the more recent data are not comparable to the data provided by the NDCHS. It is not entirely clear that any increases in annual household income can be attributed to increases in income earned from family day care.

Three studies provide information on the proportion of annual household income that comes from the family day care business income. The NDCHS

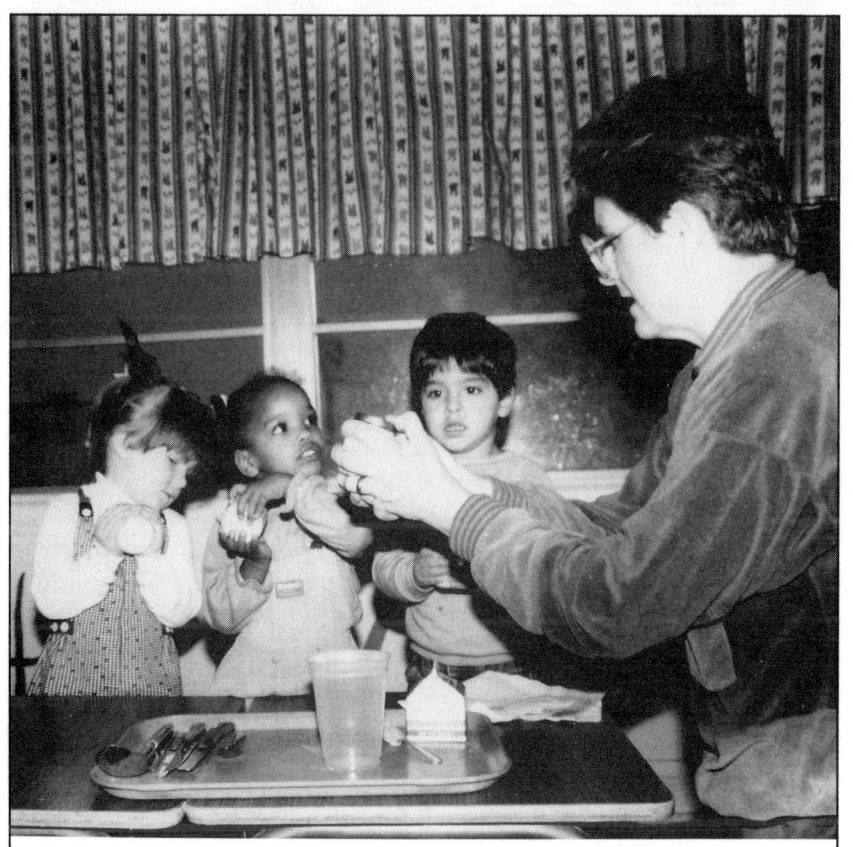

Education, training, and experience in family day care are three related factors likely to have an impact on caregiver behavior. Few providers have college degrees; most have high school diplomas and considerable experience in caring for children.

Typical providers are in their thirties or forties (with many exceptions). Most are married. Most have two or three (probably school-age) children of their own.

income data (Divine-Hawkins, 1981) reveals that the average family day care provider earned $3,844 (gross), which is 38.4% of the median annual household income reported. Kontos (1988a) reported that caregivers in North Dakota earned, on the average, 38% of their annual household income (based on the reports of the caregivers themselves). According to Fischer (1989), the average annual family day care income for caregivers in central California was $7,440, or 24% of their average household income. Taking these three studies together, we may be able to say conservatively that family day care providers typically contribute one-fourth to one-third of their annual household income.

Examining family day care income apart from household income, the data suggest that caregivers rarely earn more than $10,000 per year, even today. Emlen's early studies (Emlen et al., 1971; Emlen et al., 1974) reporting caregiver income revealed that approximately 90% of caregivers earned less than $2,000 per year, and nearly one-half (66% in one study, 41% in the other) earned less than $1,000 per year. More recently, NAEYC (1985) reported that the average annual income for a family day care provider in 1979 was $3,428, and in 1984 was $4,420. These data are consistent with those of Pence and Goelman (1987b), who found that 58% of licensed caregivers and 89% of unlicensed caregivers earned less than $5,000 annually, as well as those of Eheart and Leavitt (1986), who found that 75% of caregivers in their Illinois sample earned less than $8,000 per year. Kontos (1988a) reported that 76% of the caregivers sampled in North Dakota earned less than $10,000 per year, and 38% earned less than $5,000. One-third of the caregivers in Indiana reported an annual income of between $5,000 and $10,000, while 30% reported earning between $11,000 and $16,000 (Kontos, 1989). In California, two-thirds of family day care providers reported incomes between $1,200 and $5,000 per year, while 53% reported incomes between $5,000 and $12,000 per year (Fisher, 1989). Consistent with Pence and Goelman (1987), unlicensed caregivers were overrepresented in the lower income group, while licensed caregivers were overrepresented in the higher income group. Income differences by regulatory status were confirmed in the PCS (A Profile of Child Care Settings) study (Willer et al., 1991). Those data revealed that regulated caregivers earned $10,000 annually, on the average (50% earned less than $8,000), whereas unregulated caregivers typically earned just $1,961 per year. Caregiver reports of income must be interpreted with some caution, however, because it is not clear whether or not caregivers necessarily know how to accurately determine these figures (K. Modigliani, personal communication, December, 1990).

Most studies fail to report both gross and net income, making it impossible to determine how much of caregivers' annual income goes to expenses incurred by her business (e.g., food, insurance, toys, and equipment). The NDCHS data indicates that caregivers' net income was only 68% of gross income. In other words, caregivers spent 32% of their gross income to run their family day care business—a substantial portion of anyone's budget (see "Fees" in Chapter 4 for a discussion of the discrepancy between the cost of providing care and fees).

Overall, family day care providers appear to be members of low- and middle-income families. They supplement their family income by earning one-fourth to one-third of the total. Rarely do they earn enough to support a family.

Social support

It is easy to conjure up images of women with houses full of fussing infants and small children and little or no adult contact for the large part of each long work day. Research evidence does not support this image, however. The first study to address this issue, the NDCHS (Divine-Hawkins, 1981), did not formally assess the amount of social support. Researchers did discover, however, that caregivers did not perceive themselves to be socially isolated and believed they had sufficient contact with adults in spite of the fact that the caregivers were typically not affiliated with a child care network. Most adult contact was with friends and relatives, evidently, rather than with other caregivers. Similar findings were reported for childminders in Britain (Bryant et al., 1980).

Recently, researchers have examined in more detail the social support networks of family day care providers. Pence and Goelman (1987b, 1991), for instance, found that Canadian caregivers reported a large, diverse support network consisting of other caregivers, family, and even governmental agencies (i.e., licensing officials). Family day care providers reported larger support networks than did center-based caregivers, and unlicensed caregivers reported more contact with neighbors and less family support than licensed caregivers reported. Caregivers providing higher quality care (based on the Harms and Clifford [1989] rating scale) were more likely to report support from a family day care association than those providing lower quality care (Pence & Goelman, 1991).

In two studies using the same measure of social support, Kontos (1988a, 1989) found that caregivers perceived their social support (including family,

It is easy to conjure up images of women with houses full of fussing infants and small children and little or no adult contact for the large part of each long work day. Research evidence does not support this image, however. Caregivers do not perceive themselves to be isolated. Most adult contact is with friends and relatives.

friends, and community) to be high. In the study of North Dakota family day care providers (Kontos, 1988a), amount of social support was positively correlated with job commitment and job satisfaction but negatively correlated with job stress. Although a correlational study does not reveal causal effects, it makes intuitive sense that more social support is related to lower job stress as well as higher job commitment and job satisfaction.

In California, caregivers' informal and formal social support networks were examined (Fischer, 1989). The vast majority of caregivers had an informal support system that included someone to talk to about their caregiving experiences. Friends, other caregivers, and husbands were the most frequently mentioned members of the informal support system. The formal social support system was accessible only to licensed caregivers. This system included the county referral service, the food program, a toy/equipment lending program, and professional organizations. The referral service and the food program were the most frequently used formal supports. Affiliation with support networks was positively related to being licensed, amount of income from family day care, better business practices, and number of children in care. In other words, caregivers who were licensed, were more businesslike, served more children, and earned more money were more likely to have a larger formal support network.

Sixty suburban Chicago caregivers (30 belonging to a family day care association) reported numerous sources of social support (Jones, 1991). The most frequent sources were relatives, friends, parents, and other caregivers. As one might expect, caregivers who belonged to a family day care association were more likely to have contacts with other caregivers and to share information with them. Taking these results a step further, Mansfield (1986) found a relationship between longevity in family day care and participation in professional organizations and family day care support groups.

The research suggests that family child care providers are not socially isolated. Even unlicensed caregivers report diverse social networks. The nature of this support is probably the most important factor. It appears that the social networks of family day care providers are primarily informal, including spouse, friends, and relatives. Formal network involvement, particularly work related, seems to be somewhat contingent on licensing status or membership in a family day care association and, for all caregivers, is less available than informal network involvement (only 23% of regulated and 2% of unregulated

> *A composite picture of family day care providers suggests that they earn $10,000 or less, contributing one-fourth to one-third of their family's total income.*

caregivers belong to a sponsoring organization [Willer et al., 1991]). The correlates of social support suggest that it is an important component of a caregiver's well-being.

Professional characteristics

It is also important to characterize family day care providers with respect to their work-related background and beliefs.

Experience

It is difficult to characterize caregivers' typical level of experience in family day care. Part of the difficulty in making definitive statements regarding caregivers' experience is that the data are reported differently in different studies. Several studies reported caregivers' experience. The average experience range of caregivers in the United States was from four and one-half to seven years, indicating a relatively experienced group of caregivers (Eheart & Leavitt, 1986; Mansfield, 1986; Bollin, 1989, 1990; Kontos, 1989; Jones, 1991). The Canadian and Israeli samples were somewhat less experienced (two to three years, on the average [Rosenthal, 1988; Goelman, Shapiro, & Pence, 1990]).

Several studies found that years of experience varied somewhat with licensing status. In a sample of California family day care providers, more than one-third of the unlicensed caregivers (37.3%) but only 17.5% of the licensed caregivers had less than one year of experience; 25% of the total sample had less than one year of experience (Fischer, 1989). Approximately half of the licensed family day care providers had one to six years of experience, and a substantial number (34.9%) had seven years or more of experience. In contrast, only 18.7% of the unlicensed caregivers had seven years or more of experience. Cox and Richarz (1987) found a one-year experience difference in favor of the regulated caregivers. Pence and Goelman (1987b) also found that experience varied with licensing status in Canada. Seventy-five percent of the licensed caregivers, but only 22% of the unlicensed caregivers, had more than four years of experience.

They work 45 to 50 hours per week caring for five to eight children if they are regulated and probably fewer if they are not.

It is difficult to characterize the typical experiential background of family day care providers. It is probably safe to say that a significant minority of caregivers are relatively inexperienced (one year or less of experience), but that the majority of caregivers have more than three years of experience. It is important to remember, however, that these data may overestimate the average number of years' experience of family day care providers because the figures are based primarily on data about regulated caregivers. Four studies (Divine-Hawkins, 1981; Fosburg, 1982; Cox & Richarz, 1987; Pence & Goelman, 1987; Fischer, 1989) found that unregulated caregivers were, on the average, less experienced than were regulated caregivers.

Training

The training background of caregivers is even more difficult to characterize than is their experience. Some studies have simply focused on whether or not caregivers have received training, regardless of the type of training received. Other studies have attempted to characterize the typical type of training received by the caregivers in the sample. Still others have focused on the number of hours of training, regardless of its source and, in some instances, its content. Finally, several studies have examined caregivers' desire for or willingness to receive training rather than their actual participation in training programs.

Kontos (1988a) found that nearly three-quarters (72%) of her sample of licensed family day care providers had received some training via workshops, conferences, or high school courses, and the remaining caregivers had received some formal postsecondary coursework in early childhood education, child development, or a related curriculum (virtually none had completed a degree in these areas). The majority of this sample belonged to the Child Care Food Program and thus were required to attend workshops on a regular basis.

In an urban, more ethnically diverse sample of caregivers who were also members of the Child Care Food Program, Abbot-Shim and Kaufman (1986) found that 46% had received training via child care workshops, while 25% had taken high school courses. Peters (1972) reported that few caregivers (less than 20%) had received formal training in child care either through high school, adult education, or college. Even fewer participated in specialized training conducted by state and local agencies. In their Canadian sample, Pence and Goelman (1987b) found that most caregivers had read about or taken courses in child development (87.5% for licensed caregivers; 74% for unlicensed caregivers), but that fewer than one-third had had formal training or professional experiences in child care. Similarly, Atkinson (1988) documented that many of the caregivers in her sample had read about children or child care (81%), attended conferences and workshops (78%), or watched television programs on children (59%). Only 34%, however, reported taking formal courses on child care.

Squibb (1989) investigated training received by child care providers in Maine. More than half of the family day care providers reported reading and watching television shows or attending workshops on child care. A few had taken high school (21%) or college (27%) courses, and a substantial number had attended conferences (45%). Workshops were rated as the most useful form of training (61%).

In California, half of the caregivers in Fischer's sample reported that they had received training in child care, while only 17% reported that they had received training in family day care business management. In another study, regulated family day care providers were more likely to have received training than unregulated caregivers, but unregulated caregivers desired information on more topics (perhaps related to their lack of training [Cox & Richarz, 1987]). Sixty-five percent of the caregivers in Eheart and Leavitt's (1986) study had received no training of any kind. Childminders in Britain (Bryant et al., 1980) were most likely to have had no previous training or experience relevant to child care work (62%).

It appears that although the proportion of trained caregivers varies by locale (perhaps a reflection of opportunities), a consistent finding is that caregivers are more likely to be trained via more informal methods, such as workshops and conferences, than through formal coursework at the postsecondary level. What little formal training there is among family day care providers seems most likely to be received through high school courses.

Several researchers investigated the amount of training received by family day care providers. Bollin, in her two samples, found that the amount of training varied from an average of 21 hours (Bollin, 1990) to 45 hours (Bollin,

1989) per caregiver. In Fisher's (1989) sample of 177 caregivers of whom 50% had received some training, 44% could remember the amount and location of the training. Seventy-eight caregivers in this California sample reported attending between 2 and 792 hours of child care training offered by a variety of sponsors (schools, community agencies, churches, and associations). Of these 78, thirty had received between 11 and 69 hours of training specifically

It appears that while the proportion of trained caregivers varies by locale (perhaps a reflection of opportunities), a consistent finding is that caregivers are more likely to be trained via more informal methods, such as workshops and conferences, than through formal coursework at the postsecondary level. What little formal training there is among family day care providers seems most likely to be received through high school courses.

concerning family day care. No averages were reported for hours of training. Most of the training reported by these caregivers took place in community agencies, although colleges and universities accounted for one-fourth of the training in child care. Overall, it is difficult to make generalizations regarding the amount of training typical of family day care providers based on these varying results.

Another important factor in training beyond the amount is caregiver willingness to participate in the training. In a sample of Texas family day care providers, Aguirre (1987) found that 66% of the caregivers would like training, providing it were free. Read and LaGrange (1990) reported that 86% of the family day care providers in their study would be willing to participate in training as long as they received financial support and did not have to leave their jobs. A similar proportion of caregivers in another study believed that specialized training, not intuition and experience, was necessary for family day care providers (Jones, 1991). One-fourth of Squibb's (1989) sample of highly experienced Maine caregivers were interested in taking college courses in early childhood education, and one-third were interested in earning associate degrees. This is a substantial minority who were willing to consider formal training. Eheart and Leavitt (1986), however, reported that 52% of the caregivers in their study did not want training of any kind, a finding consistent with Peters' (1972) earlier study in which less than half of the caregivers (approximately 40%) were interested in receiving training.

A lack of interest in training on the part of many caregivers may very well have to do with their perceptions of what adequate training for family day care *is*. The NDCHS (Divine-Hawkins, 1981) reported that many caregivers believed that raising a family provided them with most of the skills necessary to be involved in family day care. Consistent with that finding, Fischer (1989) found that caregivers were most likely to name their experiences as parent, grandparent, or sibling as the best preparation for their job in family day care (42%) and were less likely to name formal training as the best preparation (19.5%). These data suggest that many caregivers believe that work in family day care is akin to mothering—a matter of natural dispositions and intuition rather than formal training (Fischer, 1989).

Nelson's interviews of caregivers in Vermont revealed that they made few distinctions between the skills of mothering versus the skills of caring for others' children; thus, training was viewed as an irrelevant issue. Nelson pointed out that by equating the skills of mothering and caregiving, family day care providers "denigrate their own (often considerable) abilities...." Devaluation or nonrecognition of caregiving skills is a logical outgrowth of the trivialization of mothering in our culture (Nelson, 1991a). Autonomy is reduced for caregivers whose ability to withstand demands from parents is weakened by lack of training in providing a professional aura and thus legitimizing their caregiving approach (Nelson, 1991).

To the extent that caregivers regard childrearing as the best preparation for family day care work, there is little incentive to seek out or value informal or formal training in family day care. Even so, several studies show that a significant number of caregivers are interested in receiving training of a certain type or under certain conditions. The actual forms, benefits of, and barriers to training will be discussed later.

Motivation

The caregivers in the NDCHS (Divine-Hawkins, 1981) most often indicated that they became family day care providers because they loved children. Is this typical? Of the nine other studies that asked caregivers why they chose family day care as a profession, three of the studies (Abbot-Shim & Kaufman, 1986; Pence & Goelman, 1987; Rosenthal, 1988) reported that the most frequent justification for entering family day care was their love of children. Five studies (Bryant et al., 1980; Majeed, 1983; Eheart & Leavitt, 1986; Nelson, 1988, 1991a; Bollin, 1989) found that staying home with their own children was the primary motivation of caregivers. Two other studies (Emlen et al., 1974; Aguirre, 1987) reported that money was the strongest motivation (earning an income and/or not having to pay others for child care). Among all the studies, these reasons were the three most frequently mentioned motivations for providing family day care; the reasons differed primarily in their rank order. Research on childminders in Britain supports these findings (Moss, 1987). Based on years of experience in recruiting and working with family day care providers, Perreault (1985) identified a typology of 11 caregiver profiles (e.g., "the experienced mother," "the babysitter," "the relative"). With several exceptions, the motivations of these 11 caregiver types are consistent with research findings.

Job satisfaction

Several studies have examined whether family day care providers like their work. Every study of caregivers' job satisfaction has found that they typically like their work (Emlen et al., 1971; Rose, 1976; Kontos, 1988a, 1989; Bollin, 1989, 1990; Jones, 1991; Rosenthal, 1991). Four studies actually quantified that satisfaction and found that caregivers were approximately midway between being neutral and being totally satisfied with their jobs (Pence & Goelman, 1987b; Kontos, 1988a, 1989; Bollin, 1990). For example, Kontos (1988a, 1989) found that, on the average, caregivers rated their job satisfaction 5.2 and 5.6, respectively, on a scale of 1 to 7 (7 = totally satisfied).

Several studies asked caregivers what they liked and disliked about their jobs. One group of family day care providers disliked "mothers who took advantage" (Emlen et al., 1974). Taking advantage consisted of bringing children in wet diapers, arriving late and requesting breakfast for the child, dropping off a child without talking to the caregiver, picking up children late, and paying late or not at all. According to Atkinson (1988), caregivers reported that their greatest satisfactions were working with the children (63%) and being home with their own children (46%). Their greatest dissatisfaction was their interactions with parents. Interestingly, feelings of isolation or "being stuck at home" were not problems for this sample of midwestern caregivers; husbands (24%) and substitutes (66%) covered for caregivers when they needed to leave. Similarly, Pence and Goelman (1987b) reported that the caregivers in their sample were most satisfied with their work with children. The difficulties that concerned the largest proportion of both licensed and unlicensed family day care providers were the jealousy of their own child (23.5% and 25.9%, respectively) and the demanding, tiring nature of child care work (25% and 25.9%, respectively). Unlicensed caregivers were particularly dissatisfied with their pay (29.6%) and children brought to day care sick (24.8%).

Eheart and Leavitt (1986) found that 46% of the family day care providers in their sample could not even name a dissatisfaction with their job. Of those who could, working conditions (hours, lack of breaks, etc.; 15%), feeling tied down (15%), and dealing with parents (19%) were most frequently mentioned. Only 63% in Eheart and Leavitt's study named a satisfying aspect of their work. The most frequently mentioned satisfaction was "being with children" (50%).

A few studies have examined the correlates of job satisfaction of family day care providers. Based on the family systems theory, Bollin (1989) predicted that job satisfaction would be positively associated with the establishment of boundaries between the caregiver's family and the family day care business and with indices of professionalism (experience, number of children in care, training), but would be negatively associated with the presence of the caregiver's own child in family day care. Contrary to expectations, job

To the extent that caregivers regard childrearing as the best preparation for family day care work, there is little incentive to seek out or value informal or formal training in family day care. Even so, several studies show that a significant number of caregivers are interested in receiving training of a certain type or under certain conditions.

satisfaction was negatively associated with training and boundary clarity (together predicting 36% of the variance in job satisfaction). The other variables were unrelated to job satisfaction. When the sample was divided by race, only hours of training predicted (negatively) job satisfaction for White caregivers, while for Black caregivers, job satisfaction was predicted (negatively) only by boundary clarity. For the sample as a whole, job satisfaction was associated with less training and more boundary clarity. In a more recent analysis of these data, Bollin and Whitehead (1991) found that the more satisfied caregivers charged less for their services and were less committed to their jobs but were more likely to perceive common values with their parent clientele.

In a study examining how North Dakota family day care providers' job attitudes (including job satisfaction) relate to caregivers' personal characteristics, program characteristics, and childrearing preferences, Kontos and Riessen (under review) reported that job satisfaction was associated with one personal characteristic: perceived social support. The more satisfied caregivers were those who perceived more social support from family, neighbors/friends, and the community. Contrary to expectations, job satisfaction for caregivers was unrelated to age, education, training, the number of children in care, or the number of infants in care. Job satisfaction was associated with one of the other job attitudes: perceived job stress, as measured by caregiver report of the frequency and intensity of various daily "hassles" involved in family day care. Caregivers who perceived more daily hassles were less satisfied with their work. Thus, job stress and social support were the two most important factors associated with job satisfaction.

In another study using measures identical to the North Dakota study, Kontos (1989) found that job satisfaction for family day care providers in Indiana was related to total number of children in care but not to caregiver education, training, number of infants in care, social support, or perceived job stress. Caregivers caring for more children were more satisfied with their jobs.

Contrary to expectations, Jones' (1991) comparisons of caregivers who were members or nonmembers of a family day care association revealed no differences in their overall levels of job satisfaction. Of the 17 satisfaction factors addressed, there were differences regarding just four. Caregivers who belonged to an association were more satisfied with their training opportunities, their ability to meet other caregivers, and encouragement from their spouse. The unaffiliated caregivers were more satisfied the children's behavior.

In sum, the research clearly shows that family day care providers like their work, although, understandably, they can name certain dissatisfactions about what they do. Moreover, it appears that job satisfaction is related to caregiver characteristics (e.g., training, boundary clarity, social support, job stress) and sometimes to characteristics of the work setting itself (e.g., fees, total number of children in care). Conclusions regarding the correlates of job satisfaction in family day care providers must be made cautiously, however, because only four studies have been conducted to date.

Job commitment

Because turnover among child care workers is a concern (Whitebook & Granger, 1989), it is important to consider whether family day care providers see their work as permanent or temporary. Turnover rates in family day care have been variously reported to be anywhere from 59% (NAEYC, 1985) to 41% (Stentzel, 1985) to 37% (in Vermont only [Nelson, 1990]). Majeed (1983) tracked family day care providers for seven months and found that there was 10% turnover among regulated caregivers during that time period and 61% turnover among unregulated caregivers. Depending on the figure, family day care could be characterized as having a similar or higher turnover rate than center-based day care, which experiences approximately 40% annual turnover of staff (Whitebook, Howes, & Phillips, 1989). Because staying home with one's own children is one of three primary motivators to becoming a family day care provider, it is logical to conclude that many caregivers consider their work temporary while their children are still at home and that high turnover is a consequence. Majeed's (1983) sample of former family day care providers indicated that most frequently they left their work due to stress and economics (the need to make more money).

The NDCHS (Divine-Hawkins, 1981; Fosburg, 1982) revealed that most caregivers (75%) perceived family day care as permanent employment. More recent research shows that although a number of caregivers regard their work as temporary, a large proportion of them see family day care as their chosen occupation. Aguirre (1987) and Bollin (1989) reported that more than one-half of the caregivers in their samples (69% and 59%, respectively) saw themselves as family day care providers permanently. Similarly, Moss (1987) suggested that in Great Britain, 60% of the childminders could be considered "career-

> *In California, affiliation with support networks was positively related to being licensed, amount of income from family day care, better business practices, and number of children in care.*

minders" as opposed to the remaining "short-termers." On the other hand, only 38% of the caregivers in Eheart and Leavitt's (1986) study planned to be in day care permanently (50% said they would continue for one to five years). Such discrepancies could be explained by many factors, including geographical differences in access to other employment opportunities.

Kontos and Riessen (under review) distinguished between two aspects of job commitment: whether family day care was the caregivers' chosen occupation and how long she planned to be in family day care. Forty-one percent of the caregivers indicated that they had chosen family day care as a profession, but only 33% said they planned to stay in it indefinitely. Almost one-half of the sample was consistent across these two aspects of job commitment: 23% said family day care was their chosen career and they planned to be in it indefinitely while 25% of the caregivers indicated that family day care was not their chosen profession and they were engaged in it temporarily. These data suggest that one-fourth to one-third of the caregivers were committed to their work indefinitely.

One study used preference for other work as an index of job commitment. Pence and Goelman (1987b) reported that only 16.7% of their licensed Canadian family day care providers preferred other work, whereas 50% of the unlicensed caregivers did. In other words, job commitment was higher among licensed than unlicensed caregivers. Another study examined stability among family day care providers (Bollin, 1990). Stability in this study was defined as a commitment to offer child care for at least two years, and thus did not represent a permanent commitment. In this study, 86% of the family day care providers were categorized as "stable." Combined with the results of the other studies, these data suggest that even though less than one-half of the caregivers may consider their work permanent, there is little evidence that a majority of caregivers are on the verge of quitting at a given time. Job commitment of a more short-term nature may be the norm. Once more, we must remind ourselves that (with the exception of Pence & Goelman, 1987b) this research was conducted exclusively with regulated family day care providers, and that job commitment is probably lower for unregulated caregivers.

Two researchers examined correlates of job commitment among family day care providers. To do this, Bollin (1990) attempted to identify differences between her samples of stable and nonstable family day care providers. The variables that most effectively discriminated between these two groups were

In other words, caregivers who are licensed are more business-like, serve more children, earn more money, and are more likely to have a larger formal support network.

presence of the caregiver's own young children at home (negative predictor), as well as job satisfaction, length of work week, and prior work experience with children (positive predictors). In other words, caregivers who did not have young children at home but who were more satisfied with their work, worked more hours per week, and had held a child-related job in the past were more likely to be classified as stable.

Kontos and Riessen (under review) examined how job commitment was related to caregivers' personal characteristics, program characteristics, and childrearing preferences. Job commitment, unlike job satisfaction, was predicted by a combination of personal and program characteristics. More committed caregivers were older, perceived more social support, and had less formal education, less specialized training, and more experience than did less committed caregivers. More committed caregivers also cared for more children full-time and involved children in more activities, but did less planning than did less committed caregivers. In addition, more committed caregivers were more satisfied with their jobs and perceived less job stress than did less committed caregivers.

Both Bollin's (1990) and Kontos and Riessen's (under review) research indicates that family day care providers' job commitment is more closely associated than is their job satisfaction with personal and program characteristics. This may well be because job satisfaction is uniformly high among the caregivers studied, whereas job commitment is more variable. A noteworthy point is that the only variable associated with job commitment in both studies was job satisfaction. Overall, the research suggests that job commitment is an important distinguishing characteristic among family day care providers. More research is needed to understand the characteristics of committed versus uncommitted family day care providers.

Summary

A composite picture of the typical family day care provider can now be drawn, with the understanding that the picture will be oversimplified. The typical caregiver is married, in her middle thirties, and has a high school diploma. She has two to three children of her own, most of whom are in school. She earns $10,000 or less, contributing one-fourth to one-third of her family's total income. She became a family day care provider because she likes to work with children, wanted to be home with her own children, and/or needed the money. She likes her work and is committed to staying in family day care, although perhaps not permanently. What she likes best about her work is her interactions with children; she least likes her interactions with parents. She does not feel isolated as a family day care provider and perceives herself as having an ample social support network. She is not formally trained but has some informal training experiences, primarily workshops and conferences. Her motivation for training is low since her work is perceived as an extension of mothering.

Implications

These descriptive data tell us much about family day care providers as a group. Caregiver characteristics (especially age, family size, and experience) suggest that adult learning models for determining the content and format of training are most appropriate. The majority of family day care providers have substantial experience with children as mothers and as caregivers. An adult learner approach to training would dictate that this experiential knowledge base is recognized and should become the basis for new knowledge. In addition, promoting the acquisition of a new, more theoretical or abstract knowledge base is best accomplished through explicit links with concrete experiences common to family day care providers.

Because family day care providers typically work alone, concerns about their level of social support are common. The available data suggest that although caregivers report extensive informal support networks, they may benefit from a higher level of involvement in formal family day care networks. Thus, agencies that regulate or sponsor family day care homes and family day care associations must maximize their outreach to family day care providers in order to make them aware of such opportunities and the benefits these agencies offer. Communities that have no family day care associations or sponsoring agencies need start-up assistance from communities that do have such facilities.

Chapter 4

What Services Do Family Day Care Providers Provide?

TO THIS POINT, WE HAVE EXAMINED the ecology of family day care and the personal and professional characteristics of family day care providers. Thus, we have an idea of what children and caregivers do in family day care and the impact these activities have on children. We also know a lot about who provides family day care. The missing link is the family day care "infrastructure." The infrastructure of family day care, together with caregiver characteristics, determines the ecology of family day care discussed in Chapter 2. In this chapter, we will examine the structural characteristics of family day care homes including number of children, fees, work hours, daily organization, and quality.

Number of children in care

Recall that the average number of children in care in the NDCHS (Divine-Hawkins, 1981; Fosburg, 1982) was three and one-half. Research conducted since that time suggests that the typical family day care provider cares for more children than the NDCHS indicates. The differences may be another reflection of the fact that most of the recent research involves licensed caregivers, whereas the NDCHS involved both regulated and unregulated caregivers.

Indeed, the NDCHS data indicate that unlicensed caregivers cared for the fewest number of children (M = 2.8 children) while licensed caregivers and sponsored caregivers cared for more (Ms = 4.0 and 4.3, respectively). The average number of children in care, as recorded in recent research, however, is higher still than for licensed and sponsored caregivers in the NDCHS. Only Emlen and his associates (Emlen et al., 1971; Emlen et al., 1974) found fewer children in care than did the NDCHS (Ms = 1.8 and 2.8, respectively), but these studies were conducted with only unlicensed caregivers in the late 1960s.

According to more recent research, the average number of children in family day care homes ranges from five to eight (Abbot-Shim & Kaufman, 1986;

According to recent research, the average number of children in a family day care home ranges from five to eight. However, it is difficult to make firm statements about typical group sizes in family day care because the variety of circumstances is great.

Eheart & Leavitt, 1986; Pence & Goelman, 1987b; Kontos, 1988a, 1989; Rosenthal, 1988; Bollin, 1989, 1990; Fischer, 1989; Glantz, 1989; Goelman et al., 1990; Willer et al., 1991). There are several exceptions to this, however. The subsample of unlicensed caregivers in the Pence and Goelman study cared for, on the average, only 4.07 children (still higher than the NDCHS average). The study of Child Care Supply and Need (Kisker et al., 1989) reported that across the three sites of the study, group sizes ranged from 2.9 to 3.4. This sample included a substantial number of unlicensed family day care providers. In Caspar, Wyoming, licensed family day care providers cared for 4.63 children, while unlicensed caregivers cared for only 2.66 (Majeed, 1983). The PCS study (Willer et al., 1991) revealed that unregulated caregivers enrolled three children, on the average. Fischer (1989) reported that unlicensed family day care providers cared for fewer children than did licensed caregivers, but separate means for each group were not reported. Instead, she reported that 60% of licensed caregivers each served four or more families compared with 27% of unlicensed caregivers. On the other hand, Cox and Richarz (1987) reported that 20% of the unregulated caregivers in their study were each caring for six to nine children. Obviously, making firm statements about typical group sizes in family day care is difficult.

In five of the studies that assessed group size, the mean number of children in care was six or more (Kontos, 1988a, 1989; Bollin, 1989, 1990; Glantz, 1989). Differences between studies in number of children in care are partially attributable to differences in licensing regulations between states. It is not surprising that caregivers in Indiana, where it is legal to care for 10 children full-time, have more children in care (M = 7.6 [Kontos, 1989]) than caregivers in Illinois (M = 5 [Eheart & Leavitt, 1986]), where it is legal to care for 8 children full-time. It is also noteworthy that in two of the studies reporting large group sizes, the sample of family day care providers were all or in large part participants in the Child Care Food Program (Kontos, 1988a; Glantz, 1989) and were perhaps more professionalized than the typical caregiver. It is also possible that some group sizes include the caregivers' own children while some do not, and it is not always possible to tell how the numbers were determined. Thus, the estimates may be inaccurate.

The data indicate that, at least for licensed family day care homes, the average number of children in care is higher than the NDCHS reported. Information on unlicensed family day care homes is inadequate to determine trends in numbers. The average number of children in family day care settings may have increased since the NDCHS because increases in the number of families needing care are occurring faster than are increases in the number of caregivers since the 1980s. Also, increasing the number of children in care is one way for family day care providers to increase income without increasing fees. Glantz (1989) suggested that caregivers view this approach to income enhancement as their only alternative because fee increases result in loss of clientele.

Fees

Unfortunately, researchers all too often neglect to ask family day care providers what fees they charge for their services. The earliest data on fees comes from Emlen et al. (1974), who reported that caregivers charged $15.43 per week. Nearly three-quarters of the families (70%) were using at least 40 hours of care per week. Sale (1973a, b) reported that her sample of 22 California family day care providers charged between $7.00 and $22.50 per week for their services. This range is similar to the one reported by Emlen et al. (1971) for data gathered at about the same time.

The average fee reported in the NDCHS (Divine-Hawkins, 1981; Fosburg, 1982) was a bit higher—$20.85—than those reported earlier, but the increase probably did not keep up with the rate of inflation in the 1970s. The most recent reports of caregiver fees were calculated per hour per child rather than per week per child. Stentzel (1985) reported that the average family day care provider charged $1.00 per hour per child. Caregivers in North Dakota were typically charging $1.22 per hour per child (Kontos, 1988a). In Iowa, caregivers were charging $1.15 per hour (Fuqua & Labensohn, 1986), while those in Indiana reported charging $1.02 per hour per child, on the average (Kontos, 1989). Several national or multisite studies found that family day care hourly fees ranged from $1.04 to as high as $1.88 (Glantz, 1989; Hofferth, 1989; Kisker et al., 1989; Willer et al., 1991). If these fees are representative, caregivers in the late 1980s charged families in the vicinity of $35.00 to $65.00 per week for full-time care, depending on the exact number of hours of care purchased. More data are needed to determine the validity of these figures.

Fees charged are not a reflection of the true cost of services. Data are hard to come by, but it looks as if caregivers charge between $1 and $2 per child per hour, usually much closer to $1.

Culkin, Morris, and Hughes (1991), through a set of case studies, conducted an economic analysis of child care in Colorado. Parents in this study using family day care paid (on the average) $199 per month for full-time care. This fee was in stark contrast to the calculated cost of providing care that ranged from $223 to $463 per month per child. These data present a clear reminder that fees are not a reflection of the true cost of services. The factor most responsible for the difference between the two figures is the "low-wage subsidy" contributed by the caregiver.

How low is that wage? Typical annual income for family day care providers was reported earlier. Willer et al. (1991) reported that regulated caregivers earned $4.04 per hour, while unregulated caregivers earned only $1.25 per hour (gross income). A recent study reported that caregivers in Wisconsin typically earned $2.37 per hour when business expenses and work hours were taken into account (Riley & Rodgers, 1989, cited in Adams, 1989). Average hourly fees have increased in the last 15 years, but only slightly (7% to 11% [Willer et al., 1991]). Nelson (1988) pointed out that fees charged by family day care providers—thus, their income—are linked to the public wage structure for women. Nelson's interviews with caregivers revealed that, as Glantz (1989) proposed, family day care providers take into account typical women's salaries when they set their fees.

Work hours

Ample evidence is available regarding the number of hours per day or per week worked by family day care providers. Simple logic tells us that a caregiver is likely to work longer than the traditional eight-hour day. If a caregiver is serving families whose work days are eight hours plus a lunch break, then the hours during which care is needed extend approximately 30 minutes before and after work, resulting in 9 to 10 hours of care per day. Caregivers who provide both daytime and evening care may conceivably work 14 to 15 hours per day; the research confirms this logic.

It appears that 45- to 50-hour weeks are the norm for family child care providers. In studies that have assessed the average hours per week worked by caregivers, the numbers range from 43 to 51 hours, with the majority of providers working 9 hours per day or more (Bollin, 1989, 1990; Fischer, 1989; Glantz, 1989; Goelman et al., 1990). Pence and Goelman (1987b) found that licensed caregivers worked longer hours (10.04 hours per day) than did unlicensed caregivers (8.96 hours per day). Study after study confirms that family day care providers have long work days. Eighty-four percent of Eheart and Leavitt's (1986) sample worked 8 to 12 hours per day. Kontos (1988a) reported that in a sample of North Dakota family day care providers, 29% worked 11 or more hours per day, while the majority of that sample (66%) worked 9 to 11 hours per day. In a sample of Vermont family day care providers, the majority (60%) worked more than 50 hours per week; only a few (15%) worked less than 40 hours per week (Nelson, 1990). The research is consistent regarding caregivers' work hours.

Planning and organization

Researchers have rarely examined how family day care providers organize and plan their day for the children. Peters (1972) found that pre-planned activities for children were the exception, observed in only 30 of 162 homes. The NDCHS (Divine-Hawkins, 1981; Fosburg, 1982) reported that sponsored family day care homes were more likely to plan and organize activities for children than were licensed or unlicensed caregivers. More recently, Eheart and Leavitt (1989) conducted intensive observations of six family day care providers (40 hours of observation over ten months) and found that five of the six caregivers rarely planned for or extended children's play activities. According to Pence and Goelman (1987b), there were relatively few differences in the activities offered by center-based day care and family day care, but they found, in general, that family day care was more likely to be organized around what happens and what is available at home and less likely to have special "outings" or activities (e.g., swimming, going to the library, cooking, visiting museums). Unlicensed caregivers were more likely to allow the children to do their own activities and to watch more television. In another study (Kontos & Riessen, under review), 41% of the caregivers reported that they planned at least one activity daily, and 23% reported that they planned activities two to four times per week. Only 13.5% indicated that they never planned activities. In that study, caregivers who chose family day care as their occupation were less likely to plan activities daily (33.5%) than caregivers who chose family day care as a temporary means of making a living (45.9%), but they rated the frequency of 15 typical activities higher than caregivers who did not choose family day care. Thus, even if committed caregivers less frequently planned activities than less committed caregivers, their children appeared to be more frequently involved in activities.

If, as some caregivers and researchers have suggested, caregiving for family day care providers is an extension of mothering (Gramley, 1990; Nelson, 1990, 1991a), the notion of planning and organizing activities for children may seem unnecessary and inappropriate. Gramley interviewed caregivers about their daily activities and discovered that women whose self-concept as a

Many caregivers plan an informal activity such as cooking, a craft project, or a simple outing at least once or twice a week; some offer a planned activity every day. Studies show that some providers rarely if ever plan an activity.

> *Most family day care providers earn well below the minimum wage per hour.*

caregiver involved a strong mother image provided unstructured, informal activities for children in a safe, nurturing environment in which housework was part of the daily routine. Several women whose self-concept as a caregiver included the teacher role were more likely to include a "learning time" in the children's day and to assume an instructional role. These women, however, were more likely to struggle with the dual identity of mother/teacher and experience what Gramley called *conflict and strain*.

The caregivers interviewed by Nelson (1991a) found the "professional model of caregiving" irrelevant. Only 24% believed that it was important to offer a "structured or planned day," and only 39% believed that it was important to offer "educational activities." In contrast to center-based caregivers, they believed their forte to be individualized attention for the children, a nurturing environment, and spontaneity. According to most of the caregivers, young children belong in an unstructured home environment.

Because structure and planning are more the hallmark of life in child care centers than in families, they may be viewed as inappropriate by those who endorse the spontaneous, "good mother" approach to family day care. Those whose ideal of family day care is closer to good center-based care than to healthy family life are more likely to appreciate structure and planning. Howes and Sakai (in press) suggest that developmentally appropriate care for toddlers may be jeopardized by the "good mother" model because this model sets up unrealistic expectations for caregivers given their working conditions and "detached attachment" relationships with the children (Nelson, 1991a). Others, however, are more comfortable with the "good mother" model (e.g., Modigliani, no date; Sale, 1973a,b). Washburn and Washburn (1985) suggested that both teacher and mother are critical roles that a caregiver is expected to fulfill "to some degree." Research is needed to determine whether or not the presence or absence of structure and planning in family day care affects children's development.

It is not surprising that little planning or organization is observed in family day care homes. A prime reason appears to be that education is perceived by caregivers and others as group- and skill-oriented and formally instructional rather than as a spontaneous, naturally occurring process embedded in the activities of everyday life (Gramley, 1990). Based on Gramley's study, caregivers appear unlikely to feel competent and satisfied with their teaching activities if these activities are perceived as different from the activities of mothering. Caregivers who understand that mothering and educating (through informal activities such as extending children's natural play) are complementary rather than mutually exclusive may be more likely to feel good about their work and may experience less conflict, however. In addition, they are more likely to understand that an educational orientation does not devalue the mothering role (Gramley, 1990). What is required is conscious reflection by caregivers on the learning potential for children of the ongoing daily activities in a family day care home. Such reflective abilities do not come naturally to everyone but can be enhanced by training and support by a knowledgeable, experienced peer or trainer.

Quality

In this section, discussion of family day care quality will be limited to describing the range of quality as it has been measured in current research and discussing several caregiver correlates of quality. The issue of quality was already discussed in an earlier chapter focusing on caregiver behavior and child outcomes.

Waite, Leibowitz, and Witsberger (1991), using data from the National Longitudinal Survey of Youth, obtained parental reports on the quality of their child's care by family day care providers. Quality indicators were based on guidelines for the Federal Interagency Day Care Regulations (FIDCR) regarding ratios, group size, and training. Results revealed that the vast majority of family day care homes met FIDCR guidelines for ratio and group sizes, according to the parents. The lowest rate of compliance was for ratios for infants (70%), while the highest was for group size for toddlers (100%). Family day care fared less well regarding compliance with training guidelines. Only one-fourth or fewer of the family day care providers were reported to have had training in early childhood education. The researchers cautioned that parental reports of training were probably less accurate than was their feedback for the other variables. Thus, these data present an overall positive picture of family day care quality views through the lens of child care regulations as reported by parents.

Six studies have measured quality in family day care with the Family Day Care Rating Scale (FDCRS [Harms & Clifford, 1989]). Use of a common instrument to measure quality provides a unique opportunity to make comparisons across studies using the same scale of measurement. The FDCRS is a 33-item scale used to rate six areas of caregiving practices: space and furnishings, basic needs, language and reasoning, learning activities, social development, and adult needs. Each item is rated on a scale from one to seven, with a score of 1 indicating inadequate practices and a score of 7 indicating excellent practices (3 = adequate; 5 = good). The rating is conducted following a minimum two-hour observation and an interview with the caregiver. The FDCRS has been shown to have high interobserver consistency and high internal consistency. Scores are associated with measures of home stimulation (Goelman et al., 1990), caregiver involvement with the children, and children's competence (Howes & Stewart, 1987).

Across the six studies that used the FDCRS to assess quality in family day care homes, the average item scores ranged from 2.9 to 4.33. In other words, the typical quality of these family day care homes fell between "just below adequate" and "not quite good" (Howes & Stewart, 1987; Pence & Goelman, 1987b; Howes, Keeling, & Sale, 1988; Fischer, 1989; Kontos, 1989; Goelman et al., 1990). Of the six studies, only one (Howes & Stewart, 1987) reported average item scores higher than 4; the remaining five studies reported scores between 2.9 and 3.7. Based on these studies, the consensus appears to be that family day care is typically "adequate" in quality and ranges from "inadequate" to "good," rarely reaching the rigorous standard of excellence set by the scale.

Several of the studies included both regulated and unregulated family day care providers (Goelman & Pence, 1987; Fischer, 1989). In each of these studies, the unregulated family day care providers were rated lower on the FDCRS than were the regulated family day care providers. In both instances, the unregulated caregivers' average item scores were less than 3, while the regulated caregivers' scores were nearly one point higher on the scale. It is tempting to conclude that unregulated caregivers are more likely than are regulated caregivers to provide care that is considered inadequate, according to the FDCRS. Nonetheless, the two studies, although suggestive, are not definitive. Additional research comparing regulated and unregulated family day care providers is needed.

It is important to know what characteristics of caregivers other than regulatory status are associated with quality. Three of the six studies using the FDCRS examined this issue. Goelman et al. (1990) found that the best correlates of family day care quality were a stimulating home environment, caregiver's number of years of experience, number of hours per week that care is provided, and amount of television viewed (the latter is a negative relationship). Fischer (1989) predicted family day care quality from a variety of caregiver characteristics. In that study, degree of affiliation with support networks, training, and years of schooling were the best predictors of family day care quality. Melnick and Fiene (1990) found no differences in family day care quality as a function of membership in a sponsoring agency. Finally, the

Based on studies, the consensus appears to be that family day care is typically "adequate" in quality and ranges from "inadequate" to "good," rarely reaching a rigorous standard of excellence.

It appears that 45- to 50-hour weeks are the norm for family day care providers. The research is consistent regarding caregivers' work hours.

only correlate of family day care quality in the Indiana study was the number of the caregiver's own children in care (Kontos, 1989).

Based on an Israeli sample of sponsored family day care providers, Rosenthal (1991) reported that number of children, experience, or amount of caregiver training were not related to quality of care as she measured it (caregiver interactions, educational program). Caregiver interactions were positively influenced by supervision, while the educational quality of the program was positively influenced by the average age of the children. Older children received better programs.

The lack of consistency in these results is probably at least partially due to examining different caregiver characteristics in each study. When there was overlap in some caregiver characteristics even across two of the three studies, however, the results were not consistent. The caregivers participating in these three studies were very diverse geographically, operated in different regulatory climates, and probably differed systematically in other ways. Thus, lack of consistency should not be surprising. At this point, the only caregiver characteristic associated with quality (as measured by the FDCRS) in more than one study is regulatory status.

Summary

The typical family day care provider works 45 to 50 hours per week caring for five to eight children if she is regulated and probably fewer if she is not. Her fee structure results in an hourly income of less than $5.00. She does not typically plan or organize her day around activities for children; her family day care environment is more home-like than center-like. The quality of care she provides is adequate.

Implications

The infrastructure of family day care is not conducive to healthy work environments for adults or to optimal care for children. The research reveals that caregivers with little or no training work long hours for low pay, caring for larger groups of children than was previously assumed. Under these circumstances, it is surely testimony to the resilience of family day care providers that they typically like their work and provide adequate (rather than poor) care for their young charges. We might expect the quality of care to increase with improvements in working conditions (Whitebook et al., 1989).

Apparently, many caregivers would benefit by learning strategies to increase their income without losing clients or increasing the group size of the children they care for. Also, giving themselves paid holidays and vacations may help alleviate the stress of poor working conditions without crimping their pocketbooks; this implies access to training and to formal support from those knowledgeable about family day care business practices. Working conditions in family day care make the cost, location, and timing of training crucial to accessibility. This issue will be discussed further in Chapter 6.

Whether caregivers should adopt a more professionalized model of family day care is still under discussion. Regardless of the conclusions drawn from these discussions, caregivers and children would both benefit if caregivers better understood the complementary nature of mothering and teaching. Future discussions of the issue of professionalization in family day care need to address differential effects of the "good mother" versus the "teacher" approach on children's development.

Chapter 5

Families That Use Family Day Care

IN THIS CHAPTER WE WILL CHANGE THE LENS through which we view family day care. Instead of examining family day care from the perspective of the caregiver, we will focus now on the parent perspective. No examination of child care is complete unless attention is given to the families using the care. As Divine-Hawkins (1981) puts it, "Parents represent the demand side of the day care equation, just as providers represent the supply side" (p. 21). Moreover, the primary childrearing environment of preschool children in child care is still the family, and, to the extent possible, parents select a child care setting to match their child's and family's needs. Thus, any effects of family day care environments on children's development are undoubtedly mediated by family characteristics (see Howes & Stewart, 1987; Kontos, 1990).

In Chapter 1, we briefly touched on the types of families being served by family day care, particularly with respect to age of the child and employment status of the mother (full-time versus part-time). In this chapter, we will take that discussion further by determining whether the characteristics of families using family day care are different from families using center-based care or other forms of care with respect to socioeconomic status, selection of child care, satisfaction with child care, and specific likes and dislikes they have of their child care arrangement. In addition, we will examine caregiver/family relationships in family day care by characterizing the frequency, amount, and topics of communication; the amount and sources of conflict; and the typical duration of care arrangements. Finally, implications for practice will be addressed.

Who are the families?

Families that choose family day care may or may not be different from families that choose other forms of care.

Socioeconomic status

If family day care is less expensive than center-based care (an assumption that is common but in doubt), then one might expect families that select family day care to be less well off than those selecting centers. Several studies have compared the socioeconomic status of families using family care day care to those using center-based care. The NDCHS (Divine-Hawkins, 1981) used a different approach by comparing the median income of families using family day care to the national median income. Family day care families were earning less than the national median income, suggesting that perhaps they were a relatively low-income group. Few studies comparing home- and center-based day care families, however, have found any socioeconomic differences between the two. Those studies that have found differences are likely not to have been conducted in the United States, and they have gotten inconsistent results. In Canada, Pence and Goelman (1987a) found that fathers of children in center-based day care had more education than fathers of children in family day care and that more single mothers with little education were using family day care than center-based day care. In Sweden, on the other hand, Lamb, Hwang, Bookstein, Broberg, Hult, and Frodi (1988) found that families using family day care had higher socioeconomic status than families using centers. The only American study to find socioeconomic differences (Clarke-Stewart, 1984) found differences in favor of center-based day care families but in only one of the two years of the study. More consistent evidence from three studies revealed no differences between families using home day care versus those using center-based day care on a variety of socioeconomic indicators

(Steinberg & Green, 1979; Pence & Goelman, 1987a; Rapp & Lloyd, 1989). Overall, there is little or no evidence that families using family day care are disadvantaged socioeconomically compared to families using other forms of care.

Satisfaction with care

Results of research are totally consistent with respect to parents' satisfaction with family day care. Parents were uniformly satisfied with their family day care home (Emlen et al., 1971; Willner, 1971; Wolfgang, 1977; Winget et al., 1982; Majeed, 1983; Fuqua & Labensohn, 1986; Atkinson, 1987; Kivikink &

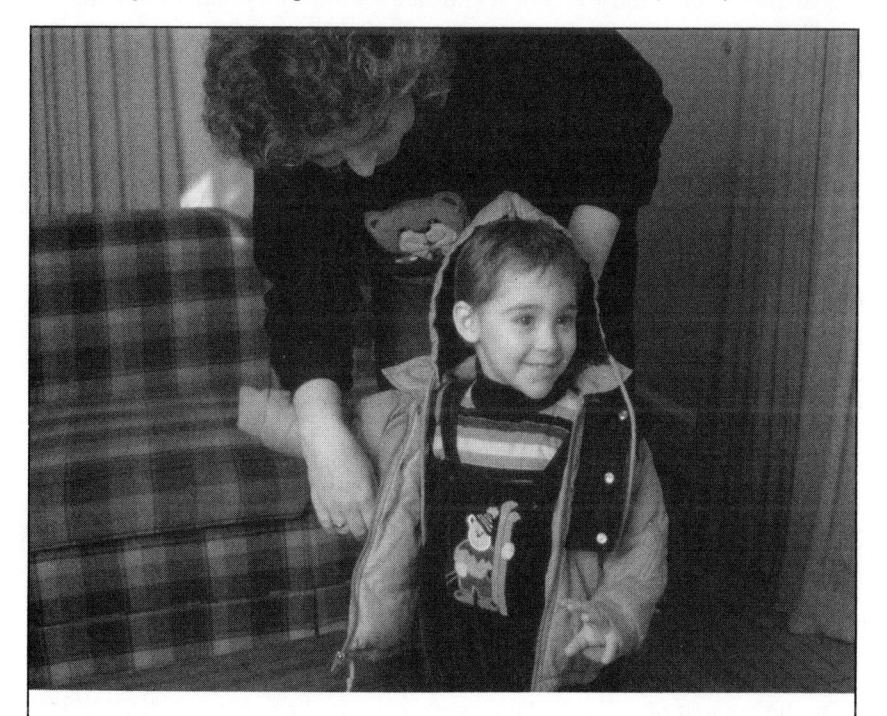

Most parents apparently do not shop around for family-based or center-based child care, gathering all the information they can get and visiting several settings. A significant number of parents place their children in day care homes sight unseen! Consumer education for parents about child care would help.

Results of research are totally consistent regarding parents' satisfaction with family day care—parents like it.

Schell, 1987; Moss, 1987; Pence & Goelman, 1987a; Fuqua & Schieck, 1989; Rapp & Lloyd, 1989; Willer et al., 1991). In studies in which parents were asked to rate their satisfaction on a numerical scale, the average rating was consistently close to the very top of the scale (e.g., an average satisfaction rating of 5.6 on a 6-point scale [Atkinson, 1987]).

The only qualifiers that might be placed on these results are that

1. there is some evidence that parents using regulated care were more satisfied than parents using unregulated care (Pence & Goelman, 1987a);

2. in spite of their high satisfaction with their present family day care arrangement, in one study 62% of parents using family day care indicated that they would choose another child care setting if they had the option, and only 38% would choose family day care again (Fuqua & Schieck, 1989); and

3. parent satisfaction with care is not necessarily an indicator of the quality of the child care setting.

As Fuqua and Schieck (1989) pointed out, parents may need to believe that their children are in good care, and dissatisfaction with their care arrangements would be inconsistent with that belief. With these qualifiers in mind, we can say that, given available choices, parents using family day care seem to be satisfied with their arrangements.

Likes and dislikes

Knowing that parents are satisfied with their family day care arrangements tells us nothing about what aspects they are actually satisfied with and what aspects they dislike or would like to change. Several studies, of which the NDCHS (Divine-Hawkins, 1981) was one of the first, asked parents about their specific likes and dislikes in addition to or instead of asking about their overall satisfaction with family day care.

Parents participating in the NDCHS were most pleased with their child's social development in family day care (over 60%) and second most pleased with the amount of individual attention their child received (50%) (Divine-Hawkins, 1981). Approximately one-third were pleased with their child's cognitive and language development, and about one-fifth liked the home-like atmosphere.

Several of these results have been replicated in other studies. In one other study (Pence & Goelman, 1987a), parents using regulated family day care mentioned positive child outcomes as a benefit of family day care (parents using center-based care also listed this as a benefit). Satisfaction with the personal attention given to their child was also frequently mentioned by another sample of parents (Winget et al., 1982). Much of what pleases parents can be attributed to the caregivers' capabilities. The other positive aspects of family day care mentioned were unique to each study.

Additional positive aspects of family day care mentioned by parents were convenience and location (mentioned by both mothers and fathers [Atkinson, 1988]), flexible hours (mothers only [Atkinson, 1988]), the caregiver (unregulated family day care only [Pence & Goelman, 1987a]), reliability, and the safe/clean and warm/loving environment (Winget et al., 1982). There appears to be little consistency across studies in what parents report they like about their family day care arrangement. This may be partially due to the open-ended nature of the questions asked of parents or could simply be a reflection of local or regional variations in the family day care settings used by the parents.

There is similar inconsistency in what parents report they dislike about their family day care arrangement. Moreover, parents typically report fewer dislikes or concerns than likes or satisfactions regarding family day care. For instance, only 50% of the parents in Atkinson's (1988) sample reported dislikes, and the dislikes reported were mentioned by just one or two parents. Also, Fuqua and Labensohn (1986) reported that only 46% of the parents in their sample reported problems in their child care arrangement, and the problems mentioned for users of family day care were the same as the problems mentioned by users of center-based day care. The most frequent concern about family day care expressed by parents in the NDCHS (Divine-Hawkins, 1981) was mentioned by only 20% of the parents. Thus, consistent with the research on parent satisfaction with family day care, parents have relatively few dissatisfactions with their care arrangement.

Just what are parents' concerns? In two studies, parents reported dissatisfaction with the type of educational experiences their child was receiving in family day care (Divine-Hawkins, 1981; Winget et al., 1982). Pence and Goelman (1987a) found that parents using family day care were more likely to report concern about their child's emotional well-being and their own guilt and less likely to be concerned about peer influences on their child than parents using center-based care. Interestingly, two aspects of family day care that were frequently mentioned in one study as positive aspects were also mentioned by other parents in the same study as dislikes: safety/ cleanliness of the environment and amount of personal attention received by the child (Winget et al., 1982). This may be a reflection of the wide variability in the family day care environments available or of differences in parents' conceptions of what constitutes good family day care.

Parents' child care problems reported by Fuqua and Labensohn (1986) were not specific to a particular type of child care or to a particular setting. Parents in this study were most concerned with finding care when their child was sick, finding infant care, and finding affordable child care. Perhaps the most negative view of family day care was reported by Willner (1971). Parents in this urban sample regarded family day care as custodial care and a stopgap until center-based care was available. These same parents reported being satisfied with their child care arrangements. Obviously, their expectations were extremely low.

The research on parents' likes and dislikes about their family day care arrangement suggests that parents can express more positive aspects than negative aspects. The lack of consistency regarding the exact nature of these likes and dislikes makes it difficult to characterize them. Perhaps we need a better way to gather this type of information from parents.

Selection of family day care

Process. Several studies of families' child care search processes have focused specifically on family day care users. Fuqua and Labensohn (1986) found that the information sources used by parents in their search did not vary by type of care selected (center- versus home-based care). Families were most likely to use friends and neighbors as sources of information (77%) and somewhat less likely to use advertisements in newspapers and telephone books (43%). The majority of families used one (45.5%) or two (33.35%) sources of information.

The search process for childminders in Britain is quite similar to the reported search process in the United States (Bryant et al., 1980; Moss, 1987). Parents

How much do family day care providers and parents talk with each other, and about what?

in Britain most frequently find their children's minders via friends and neighbors. A substantial minority (approximately 30%) located their minders via government health or welfare office referrals. British parents reported using advertisements to locate childminders even less than did American parents (5% to 10%).

Other studies of the child care search process (independent of type of care) support these findings that informal sources of information are the resources most frequently used by parents using family day care (Powell, 1980; Kisker et al., 1989; Willer et al., 1991). Parents much less frequently relied upon newspaper advertisements, according to results of the Child Care Supply and Needs Study (Kisker et al., 1989), and community agencies (e.g., resource and referral) were used less than 5% of the time in each of the three target communities. Powell (1989) concluded that parents began their child care search by consulting members of the nuclear family and close friends and then, if necessary, branched out to peripheral ties in the community (e.g., relatives, associates at work).

Fuqua and Schieck (1989) compared users of family day care who worked with a child care resource and referral program when selecting child care versus those who did not. As expected, they found that parents who had access to resource and referral services based their decision on more reliable information, spent more time looking for child care, and visited more settings. On the other hand, both groups of parents rated themselves as equally prepared to select child care and were equally satisfied with the care they chose. These data suggest that parents' and professionals' conceptions of preparedness for the child care search process are different, something that may also hold true for users of center-based day care.

An important aspect of how families select child care is the extent to which parents "shop around." In one study, families using centers were more likely to have visited the facilities prior to placing their children (88%) than were families using family day care (69% [Rapp & Lloyd, 1989]). These results were nearly identical to those of Fuqua and Labensohn (1986), who reported that 89% of parents using centers had visited them prior to placement, while only 68% of the families using family day care had done so. Fuqua and Labensohn suggested three reasons why parents may be reluctant to visit family day care homes:

1. reluctance to "inspect" the private home of a stranger;

2. reluctance to be perceived as not trusting a potential caregiver, particularly if child care is scarce and/or parents need to establish rapport with the caregiver; and

3. a tendency not to view purchasing child care from a family day care provider as a business arrangement.

To what extent do parents contact multiple caregivers prior to selecting a child care arrangement? In Britain, Bryant et al. (1980) found that 40% of the parents using childminders had selected the only minder whose name was given to them. For most of the remaining parents, the minder they selected was the only one they contacted during their search, even though they were given more than one name. Moss (1987) suggested that this pattern is not necessarily

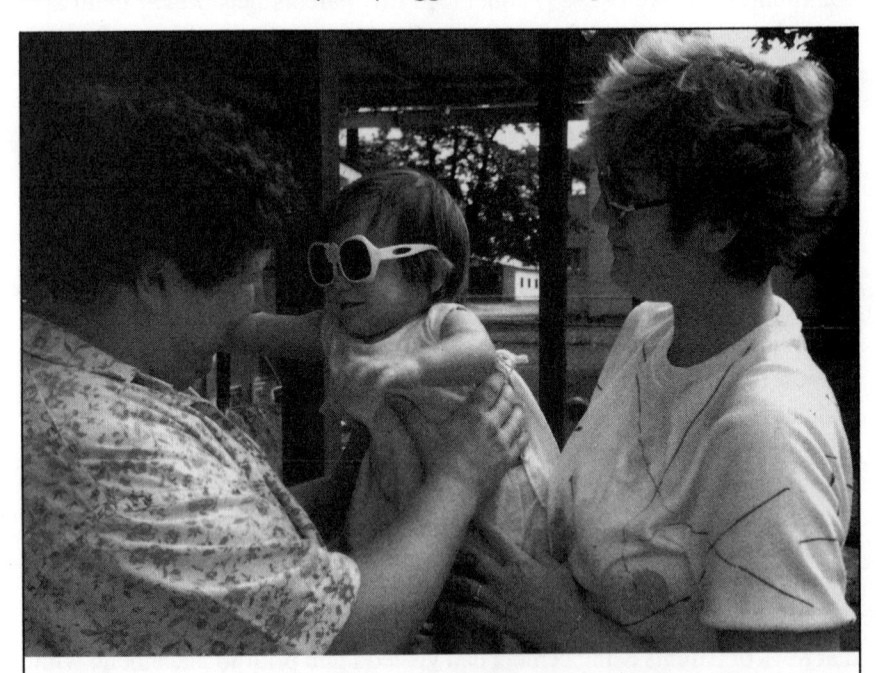

The intentions of both parents and caregivers to communicate with each other seem to be good, but substantive subjects pertaining to the child or the care are in most instances probably not discussed. Training for family day care providers regarding working with parents would be beneficial to both parties.

maladaptive because, in a number of cases, the mothers already knew the minder. Other disincentives to making multiple contacts with minders may be the time spent away from work, the impracticality for mothers of young children to "haul them around" to many homes, and lack of support for the process by social service agencies (Moss, 1987). The implication is that, given the context, parents' search strategies represent the best that they can do under the circumstances.

"Shopping" for child care appears to be equally unlikely in the United States. Approximately one-half of the parents in the National Child Care Supply and Need Study (Kisker et al., 1989) reported considering caregivers other than the one they chose during the selection process. Consistent with that finding, the average time spent searching for child care was quite limited (one-half day or less). These results are based on parents using a variety of child care forms, not just family day care.

The research on how families select family day care is not plentiful. It does suggest, however, that there are some important similarities and differences between the selection processes for family day care and for center-based day care. Although the majority of parents visit the child care site prior to placing their child, it is noteworthy that nearly three times as many parents selecting family day care as parents selecting center-based day care fail to make such a visit. It is certainly an issue for concern if nearly one-third of family day care users place their children site unseen! Another concern, even for parents who do visit a potential child care site, is the lack of comparison shopping that is evident in parents' search strategies.

Criteria. By examining the criteria parents use for selecting family day care, we can begin to understand parents' notion of what good day care is. Several patterns emerge from the results of research concerned with this issue. The criterion most consistently reported concerned caregiver abilities or characteristics (Emlen et al., 1974; Rothschild, 1978; Divine-Hawkins, 1981; Majeed, 1983; Pence & Goelman, 1987a; Kisker et al., 1989; Willer et al., 1991)—more specifically, cognitive and language stimulation, child orientation, training, quality, and "better care." The second most consistently reported criterion concerned the logistics of child care, such as hours (Emlen et al., 1974; Rothschild, 1978; Majeed, 1983), location (Emlen et al., 1974; Divine-Hawkins, 1981; Majeed, 1983; Kisker et al., 1989), cost (Emlen et al.,

One researcher's results lead her to conclude that built-in differences of need, interest, and viewpoint make it likely that many parent-provider relationships will include some conflict.

1974; Divine-Hawkins, 1981; Kisker et al., 1989), and reliability (Willner, 1971; Divine-Hawkins, 1981; Atkinson, 1988). Parents look for family day care with flexible hours that is close to home or work, does not require frequently locating substitute care, and is affordable. Other criteria for selecting family day care that are reported in at least two different studies include a caregiver with similar values (Wolfgang, 1977; Atkinson, 1988; Zinsser, 1990) and a home-like setting (Rothschild, 1978; Pence & Goelman, 1987a).

There is evidence that family day care is preferred by some parents because it is perceived to more closely replicate home care with mother than center-based care. For instance, Rapp and Lloyd (1989) found that mothers who adhere to the "home as haven" ideology are more likely to choose family day care than center-based care. The "home as haven" perspective is based on the notion that a mother is the only person who can provide "refuge" to her family. Working mothers who adhere to this perspective may use family day care more heavily than they use center-based care in order to reduce the dissonance between their beliefs and their behaviors (Rapp & Lloyd, 1989). Along these same lines, Steinberg and Green (1979) reported that parents using family day care perceived more congruence between their values and their caregivers' than did parents using center-based day care or in-home care. In her interviews with parents using informal, unregulated family day care, Zinsser (1990) found that parents were looking for care that most closely resembled their own upbringing. Thus, for these parents, a quality child care arrangement involved care within the family or, if that was not possible, within the neighborhood.

Although a variety of criteria for selecting family day care surface in the research, several factors appear to be more salient than others. Understandably, parents seem to view the caregiver as a key ingredient for good child care. The other major concerns all involve the logistics of child care—reliability, location, cost, and hours. Without these latter four factors favorably in place, the child care arrangement does not meet the needs of the parent. Without a good caregiver, the needs of the child are not met. Thus, from the parents' viewpoint, these five factors are critical for a successful child care arrangement. These factors vary little or not at all from criteria for the selection of center-based care. Parents' desires for a home-like setting, however, are obviously unique to family day care.

Parent/caregiver relationships

An important aspect of any early childhood program is the relations between parents and caregivers (Powell, 1989).

Communication

Few studies have examined communication patterns between parents and family day care providers. Most studies on this topic focus solely on providers in centers. In one of the studies involving family day care, Hughes (1985) compared the extent and nature of parent-caregiver interactions between home- and center-based care for the purpose of understanding the "informal help-giving" of day care providers. Results of this study were based on interviews with 73 caregivers (35 family day care providers) but no parents. According to the caregivers, those in centers talked with more parents each week (average = 6.8) than those in homes (average = 3.1). This significant difference reflected the differences in enrollments between centers and homes. The amount of time caregivers spent with parents was also different. Caregivers in homes reported spending 54.7 minutes per week with each parent while those in centers reported spending only 13.7 minutes per week with each parent. Consistent with this difference, caregivers in homes reported spending more total time per week with parents (170.9 minutes per week) than did caregivers in centers (54.7 minutes per week). The differences in overall time spent with parents as reported by the caregivers indicate that family day care providers' additional time with parents is not just a result of having fewer parents with whom to interact.

The frequency with which problems of varying severity were discussed did not vary as a function of home- versus center-based care. Family day care providers rated the frequency with which problems were discussed on a scale from *never* to *very often*. They reported *sometimes* discussing serious and very serious concerns with parents. Typical concerns or problems and routine topics were discussed less than *often* but more than *sometimes*. The childrearing concern most likely to be discussed was physical health and growth, and concerns least likely to be discussed were family day care home policies and television watching. The remaining concerns (e.g., nutrition, learning, discipline, behavior problems) were discussed *some of the time* by family day care providers. Parents' personal concerns were less likely to be discussed than childrearing concerns. The most frequently discussed parent concern was their jobs, while the least frequently discussed parent concern was problems with their spouses.

Family day care providers' most frequently reported responses to parents' concerns were to

1. ask questions,
2. share personal experiences, and
3. offer sympathy.

Education and experience were apparently associated with different patterns of response by caregivers, however. More educated caregivers offered more sympathy and were less likely to just listen, to tell the parents to count their blessings, or to point out the consequences of bad ideas. Less experienced caregivers offered less sympathy but more often told the parent to count his or her blessings, pointed out the consequences of bad ideas, or tried to help the parent solve his or her own problem.

In response to their interactions with parents, caregivers most frequently reported feeling supportive, encouraging, personally satisfied, sympathetic, and puzzled. Hughes suggested that these data support the assumption that day care providers are an important source of information and support for parents' child-related concerns. What we do not learn from this study is how caregivers' "help-giving" affects parents nor how closely caregiver reports of communication with parents match their actual behavior.

Another study of parent-caregiver communication involved interviews and observations of both parents and family day care providers (Leavitt, 1987). Interviews were held with 31 caregivers, followed by 20 two-hour visits made to 6 of the 31 family day care homes across a 10-month period. Finally, 17 parents from the 6 observed family day care homes were interviewed.

Parent interviews revealed that the parents believed that talking with their family day care provider was important and that most of their conversations focused on children. Parents and caregivers were in agreement regarding the focus of their conversations but were not in total agreement regarding how much time they spent communicating with one another. More than one-half of the parents (53%) reported talking to the caregiver "up to 20 minutes per day." The largest proportion of caregivers, however, indicated that the amount of time spent talking to parents "varied." Observations conducted during arrival and departure times allowed comparisons to be made between parent and caregiver reports of amount and topics of communication.

The observations revealed that parent-caregiver communication during arrival and departure times was brief and not very informative. The information exchanged, as reported, did tend to focus on the child. Leavitt (1987) indicated that the conversations were not particularly informative, typically offering only a brief comment on the child's day, the child's health, or the child's progress in toilet training. Some caregivers were rarely observed initiating conversations with parents and, when parents initiated them instead, the caregivers' responses were limited (e.g., one word responses to questions). Sometimes interactions between parents and caregivers were limited because parents were rushed, leaving little opportunity for either individual to initiate a conversation. Overall, Leavitt found the actual interactions between parents and caregivers to be less desirable than reported.

Zinsser (1990) reported that parents and caregivers in her study communicated very little about the child. This lack of communication was attributed to the fact that both parents and caregivers viewed the child care arrangement as custodial, limiting relevant topics to reports of daily routines. Zinsser suggested that this is also a way to reduce potential conflict.

The study of childminding in Britain (Bryant et al., 1980) focused a bit on parent-caregiver communication. The parents in that study perceived ample opportunities to talk with minders about their children. The minders themselves were not as satisfied; 40% of them desired increased communication with parents. When asked whether they had communicated the previous day, parents and minders revealed that communication may not have been as "ample" as parents perceived it to be. Fewer than one-half of the parents (46%) had talked with the minder the previous day. In general, the interviews suggested that communication was not a problem for parents or minders when things were going well (this was the case for approximately 30% of the families). When there was a problem with the child, communication was a problem about half of the time. Thus, in the majority of instances, parent-minder communication was perceived to be adequate.

It is difficult to draw conclusions about parent-caregiver communication on the basis of three such different studies. Parents' and caregivers' intentions to effectively communicate appear to be good. Leavitt's (1987) observations lead us to doubt whether these intentions are really enacted. The results of Bryant et al. (1980) suggest that communication may be a problem approximately one-third of the time. More observational research as well as interviews with parents and caregivers are necessary before we can make definitive statements about the nature of parent-caregiver communication in family day care settings.

Conflict

This is another aspect of parent-caregiver relationships about which there is very little information specific to family day care. Several studies that have focused on potential problems between parents and family day care providers can inform us, if somewhat indirectly, on this topic.

Nelson (1989) interviewed family day care providers and the mothers who use their services to gain insight into the relationship between them. She discovered that there were "significant ideological differences between the two groups which retarded mutual understanding" (p. 11). Family day care providers in her sample had very traditional values regarding the role of women and the importance of motherhood. They could not understand how a mother could leave her child in someone else's care. The mothers, on the other hand, expressed some ambivalence about leaving their children but believed that economic necessity and the selection of good child care justified their sacrifice. They could not imagine caring for "all those children" all day. Each of the groups felt somewhat powerless in the face of the other, and this was complicated by the fact that they entered into the relationship with different interests. Caregivers want to limit the time they spend caring for the children of others and to be adequately paid for their services. Mothers want to pay as little as possible and to have some control over childrearing. Thus, the interests of caregivers and mothers are bound to interfere with one another. Nelson suggests that the abuses that occur in mother-caregiver relationships are a result of attempts to "make the best of an unmanageable situation." Moreover, she goes on to say that problems will continue to occur unless significant social change occurs, particularly regarding the resources available for and respect given to child care, to the structure of waged work, and to the domestic division of labor. This sociological analysis complements the more psychological interpretations of parent-caregiver relations provided by other researchers.

Emlen et al. (1974) reported that among the 60% of mothers in their sample that expressed some dissatisfaction with their family day care arrangement, one of the primary reasons for dissatisfaction was mother and/or caregiver anger, resentment, or disapproval of the other's behavior. Taking the other perspective, Atkinson (1988) found that caregivers' most commonly mentioned problems with providing family day care involved interactions with parents. The negative interactions most frequently concerned late or partial payments (34%), general inconsiderateness (19%), and failure to pick up children on time (12.5%). On the other hand, Leavitt (1987; Eheart & Leavitt,

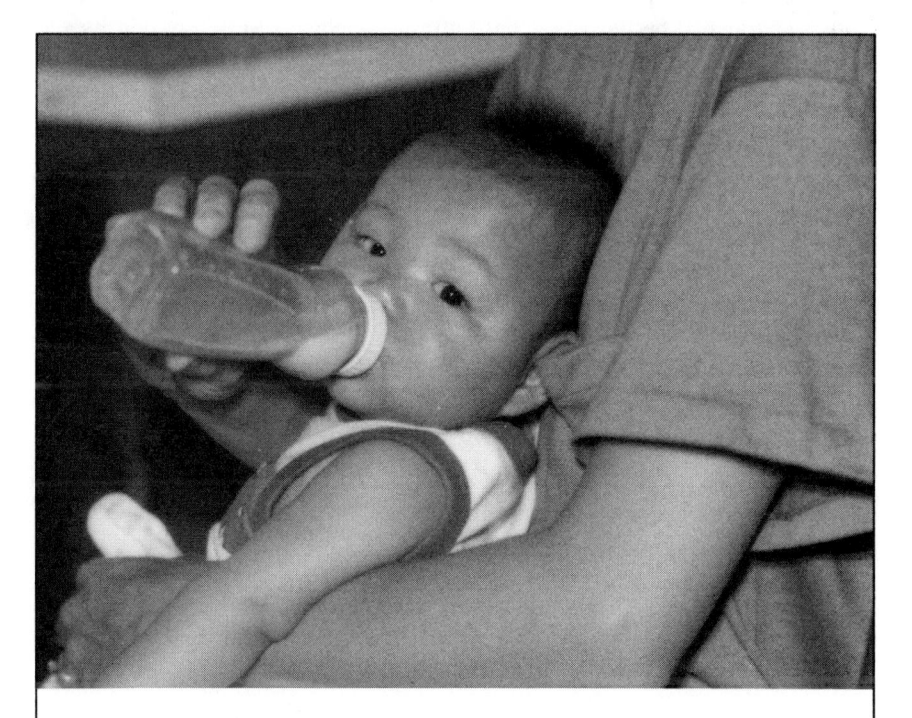

Without significant social change—particularly regarding the resources available for and respect given to child care, to the structure of waged work, and to the domestic division of labor—problems between parents and caregivers will probably continue to occur.

The frequency with which caregivers expressed negative attitudes toward parents led one researcher/observer to question the extent to which caregivers are as supportive, sympathetic, and encouraging as they believe they are.

1986) received more positive reports from both parents and caregivers in two separate studies. In the earlier study that surveyed 150 family day care providers, only 10% indicated that dealing with parents was one of the least satisfying aspects of their jobs. In the more recent study, parents expressed few criticisms of their children's caregivers and were very satisfied with the quality of care their children were receiving. During the interviews of 31 caregivers, however, only 26% said they had no problems with parents. The majority reported problems with parents regarding payment, scheduling, ill children, and personality conflicts.

Observations of six caregivers failed to reveal the conflicts or disagreements with parents reflected in the interviews (Leavitt, 1987). What they did reveal, however, was critical or resentful attitudes on the part of the caregiver toward the parents. These attitudes seemed to be elicited by the caregivers' perceptions of being taken advantage of and by disagreements with parents' childrearing practices, especially if these practices made the caregivers' job harder. The frequency with which caregivers expressed these negative attitudes toward parents led Leavitt to question the extent to which caregivers are as supportive, sympathetic, and encouraging toward parents as Hughes (1985) reports.

A review of British childminding research revealed that minders tended to be critical of the parents they served (Moss, 1987). One-half to two-thirds of the caregivers in several studies reported difficulties with parents. Primary bones of contention were money, hours, feelings of being used, and differing opinions on child care. Parents, on the other hand, were less critical of minders than vice versa and seemed unaware of the minders' criticisms of parents. Moss suggested two factors that may lead to parent-minder conflict. One factor is the frequency with which childminders are antagonistic to the notion of women working outside the home; the other factor is the frequency of ambiguous and imprecise child care arrangements that may lead to conflicting expectations on the part of parent and minder.

It appears that, as in center-based settings (Kontos & Wells, 1986), relations between parents and caregivers in family day care are potentially problematic. The potential for problems may be heightened by the greater intimacy and informality of the home setting compared to a center. The research cannot tell us what effect of parent-caregiver conflict has on the quality of care or on the child.

When selecting family day care, parents are most concerned with the caregiver's characteristics and/or abilities, and with the logistics of the setting (hours, locations, reliability).

Duration

One interesting aspect of parent-caregiver relationships is how long they last. Many studies report the length of time a currently enrolled child has been in the family day care setting. Due to the rarity of longitudinal studies, however, very little is known about how long a child care arrangement typically lasts. Emlen et al. (1974) reported that the typical (median) family day care arrangement in their study lasted only 13.5 weeks. The range was from less than one week to more than two years, but three-quarters of the child care arrangements lasted less than six months. It is hard to imagine that these data are representative, especially because the family day care arrangements in this study were primarily with unlicensed caregivers, many of whom were friends of the mothers (interestingly, arrangements with friends were shorter term than those with strangers). A more recent report based on data from the early 1970s (Floge, 1985), however, found that of the women who were still working or attending school after a 12-month interval between interviews, only 50% of those using family day care were still using the same child care arrangement. This number was consistent with the average across all types of child care arrangements. Floge concluded that, given the frequency with which mothers change their arrangements, most child care is temporary; the study by Emlen et al. appears to support that conclusion. Data from the British study of childminding are a bit more optimistic, however (Bryant et al., 1980). In that study, 38% of the children had been with their current minder for 12 months or longer. An additional 30% had been with their minders for 6 to 11 months. No matter what the source of information, it appears that longevity is not the hallmark of family day care arrangements. The data base is inadequate for drawing firm conclusions, however.

Summary

At this point, we have no evidence that families who use family day care are different socioeconomically than families who use other forms of care. Like most families who use child care, they are extremely satisfied with their child care setting, although there is reason to qualify this assessment based on some inconsistencies in parents' reports. Parents more readily report what they like about their family day care arrangements than what they dislike. There are few consistencies in the reports of what they like and dislike, however. The search process for family day care seems to very closely resemble the search for center-based day care, except that parents tend not to visit family day care settings prior to enrolling their child. When selecting family day care, parents are most concerned with the caregiver (characteristics and/or abilities) and with the logistics of the child care setting (hours, location, and reliability). Parental and caregiver reports suggest that they both value communication and regularly communicate with each other about the child. Observational studies, however, lead us to question whether these good intentions are put into action. Caregivers, but rarely parents, regularly report conflict, which frequently concerns payment, scheduling, and the like. Observations failed to confirm overt conflict but did reveal caregivers' negative attitudes toward parents. Clearly, the potential exists for problems between parents and family day care providers. Finally, two studies suggest that family day care arrangements are short in duration.

Implications

The research reviewed on parents suggests that two things are needed:

1. consumer education for parents about child care, and
2. training for family day care providers regarding working with parents.

These two strategies could help parents and caregivers to better understand and appreciate one another's perspectives. Parents need effective child care search strategies (that include visitation) and an understanding of caregivers' needs for adequate pay and regular, limited hours. In effect, they need to perceive of purchasing family day care services as a business arrangement, even though it takes place in a home. Caregivers need to understand and support working mothers and to have appropriate expectations for their behavior. Caregivers must also learn to effectively communicate with parents under less-than-ideal circumstances (i.e., at arrival and departure times). The hostility that caregivers feel toward parents may result from unexpressed concerns and frustrations that parents—if they were aware of the concerns and if they respected their caregiver—could help to resolve. Caregivers must be assertive and articulate to overcome this problem, however, and these are skills with which many people need assistance.

Chapter 6

Licensing and Accreditation

THE REGULATORY CLIMATE IN EACH STATE is likely to influence the quality and availability of child care. For center-based child care, the assumption has been that the more stringent the regulatory standards, the higher the minimum or "floor" of quality (Phillips, Lande, & Goldberg, 1990). For family day care, however, some individuals suggest that stringent regulation actually may be a disincentive to become regulated and thus may not have the intended effect (Children's Foundation, 1989). Although most center-based child care programs are regulated, estimates suggest that only 10% to 40% of family day care providers are regulated (Kahn & Kamerman, 1987). Willer et al. (1991) reported that between 10% and 18% of family day care providers are regulated. These figures do not offer proof that family day care regulations are unrealistically stringent because there are numerous other explanations (e.g., parents' and caregivers' knowledge about the existence of regulations, attitudes toward governmental regulation, the number of caregivers who may be legally unregulated due to small group sizes, lack of enforcement, and so forth). The figures do suggest, however, that current regulatory systems applied to family day care may be dysfunctional. Regulations subject to widespread lack of compliance or enforcement fail to serve their function of protecting young children from harmful conditions of care. This chapter will examine the types of regulation currently in place for family day care as well as what is regulated and future directions for family day care regulation. In addition, evidence regarding caregivers' views of regulation will be reviewed.

Differences between regulated and unregulated caregivers will not be addressed in this chapter because that information is woven into the other chapters. Finally, another aspect of quality control designed to promote optimal levels of care on a voluntary basis—rather than minimum levels required by licensing—will be addressed: accreditation. Several methods of accreditation for family day care providers will be compared and contrasted.

At present, twenty-six states limit caregivers to either two or (in some states) three infants. It is hard to give warm, responsive care to more than this number of babies. Thirty-three states have a five- or six-child (of any age) limitation, although 10 states have a higher limit. Seven states exempt from regulation caregivers who care for five or fewer children.

Regulation

Types of regulation

The 1990 Family Day Care Licensing Study conducted by the Children's Foundation (1990) found three primary forms of regulation for family day care. The predominant form used exclusively by 21 of the 50 states (plus the District of Columbia) is *licensing*. Licensing is voluntary in only one state. States that opt for licensing set minimal standards that must be met by caregivers prior to providing services, grant formal permission to provide services based on adherence to those standards, and have the authority to ensure that standards continue to be met (via monitoring).

The form of regulation used exclusively by 16 of the states is *registration* (in three states, registration is voluntary), which differs from licensing in the following ways: (1) the state does not guarantee that family day care homes meet its standards, and (2) routine inspections are not performed. Instead, caregivers "self-inspect" and sign a statement indicating that they are aware of the standards and believe they are in compliance with them. In addition, parents are given a copy of the standards and, it is hoped, procedures for filing a complaint. Inspections are made when complaints are received and, in some states, on a random basis for a certain proportion of the registered caregivers. A simplified form of registration involves a sign-in procedure whereby all caregivers are listed with the regulatory agency but are not required to meet any standards. Proponents of this simplified form of regulation believe that just identifying the family day care providers is a significant step and that universal compliance with this type of regulation is a realistic goal (Morgan, 1980).

The third form of regulation, *certification*, has been chosen exclusively by only five states. According to the Children's Foundation (1990), certification is basically the same as registration but is typically linked to caregivers receiving public funds. For instance, in two of the states using certification (Arizona and Ohio), caregivers required to be certified are those serving subsidized children (Arizona) or receiving public funds (Ohio). Two additional states have chosen what they call *self-certification*, which is not tied to funding.

Research findings suggest that current regulatory systems applied to family day care may be dysfunctional.

Of the remaining states, five use a combination of two of the previously mentioned three forms of regulation, and three have requirements that do not fall into these three categories. In the latter situation, for instance, Louisiana requires alternate approval of all family day care providers who participate in the Child Care Food Program, and caregivers caring for six or fewer children are unregulated. Those caring for more than six children are considered a center and are subject to a separate set of regulations. How states regulate family day care is highly individual.

What is regulated

In spite of the individuality of states' regulations, there is some consistency in the aspects of family day care that are regulated. The Children's Foundation (1990) grouped regulations into six categories in their Family Day Care Licensing Study: regulations and requirements (e.g., who must be regulated, maximum group size, liability insurance, space, inspections, and so forth), training and orientation, caregiver qualifications, discipline, zoning, and sick child care.

Regulations and requirements. Typically, who must be regulated is determined by a minimum number of children, and those caregivers who are regulated must adhere to a maximum allowable group size. Additionally, some states specify a caregiver/infant ratio. Twenty-six states limit caregivers to either two or three infants (defined differently by different states). A recent analysis of child care regulation found that the median enrollment limitation for family day care homes was six (Phillips, Lande, & Goldberg, 1990). According to this analysis, 8 states have a 5-child limitation, 28 states and the District of Columbia have a 6-child limitation, and 10 states exceed these limitations and in one case go as high as 16. Fourteen states exempt caregivers who care for fewer than a designated number of children. Of these 14 states, 4 exempt caregivers with just one or two children; 3 states, with up to three children; 3 states, with up to four children; and 4 states, with up to five children. Thus, many caregivers are legally unregulated in these 14 states, particularly the 7 states that exempt caregivers with up to four or five children. The remaining states either allow more than three infants or have no limits.

Regulations subject to widespread lack of compliance or enforcement fail to serve their function of protecting young children from harmful conditions of care.

Space requirements are included in 36 (72%) states' regulations. Most of these states (26) require 35 square feet of indoor space and varying amounts of outdoor space; the remaining 10 of these states have unique space requirements (Children's Foundation, 1990). The other 15 states have no space requirements.

The nature (announced versus unannounced) and frequency of monitoring visits are frequently addressed by state regulation and vary considerably from state to state. Liability insurance is a relatively recent area to be addressed by regulations and is dealt with by only 11 states.

Caregiver qualifications. Eighty-four percent of the states require family day care providers to be at least 18 years of age; the remaining states require them to be 19, 20, or 21 years of age. In two states, the maximum age is also indicated (age 70 in Arkansas and age 71 in Washington, D.C.). Thirty-nine states require caregivers to have a physical examination and/or a TB test, while 13 states require none. The majority of states (36) now require criminal history checks, fingerprinting, or screening through the Child Abuse Registry. Three additional states also require this information, but only under certain circumstances.

Training and orientation. Eleven states require attendance at an orientation session; 15 states do not require such attendance, although it may be available in certain areas. The remaining 25 states make no mention of orientation in the regulations. With respect to training, 29 states have some type of requirement, ranging from training in CPR or first aid to courses in child development. Typically, states simply indicate that a certain number of hours of in-service training per year are required without specifying content. Twenty-two states have no training requirements for family day care providers. Six states require both training and orientation.

Zoning. The Children's Foundation (1989) has expressed concern about this issue because in many localities, child care is not dealt with as "customary home use" by the zoning ordinances (Morgan, 1980). A few states consider family day care to be residential use of property (eight), have made family day care exempt from zoning ordinances (two), or allow special-use permits for family day care homes (one). The majority of states (36) presently require that family day care homes comply with local zoning ordinances (Children's Foundation, 1990). Consequently, family day care homes, regarded as businesses in residential settings, frequently must operate outside the law.

Discipline. The regulations regarding discipline focus on the use of corporal punishment (sometimes referred to as physical punishment or spanking). Only three states do not address the issue at all. Of the remaining states, the vast majority (39) prohibit it. Four states allow corporal punishment, and five states allow such punishment under certain conditions (e.g., parental permission, if the child is over the age of five).

Sick child care. This is the regulation category addressed by the fewest states. Twenty-two states have regulations regarding sick child care, indicating the conditions under which children must be isolated, removed, or otherwise dealt with. Seven additional states are developing regulations for sick child care.

Future directions for family day care regulation

Several child care advocates have questioned the appropriateness of current child care regulatory approaches and recommended considering more innovative approaches than the traditional licensing model (Class, 1980; Morgan, 1980; Phillips et al., 1990). No one questions the need to safeguard the health and safety of young children. With so few family day care providers regulated, what is being questioned is whether the safeguards are actually in place, whether regulations for family day care serve the same functions as they do for center-based day care, and whether enforcing family day care licensing is feasible. The Children's Defense Fund (Adams, 1990) believes that the current approach to family day care regulation leaves many children unprotected—without "assurances of adequate supervision and quality child care."

From a sheerly practical standpoint, 100% compliance to family day care licensing regulations is probably an unrealistic goal given the number of caregivers affected, the low visibility of homes (compared to centers), high turnover of caregivers and children, and the informal nature of much of family day care. The cost of monitoring alone would be astronomical and thereby prohibitive. To remain economical and limit work loads for licensing staff, states have tolerated (either intentionally or by default) high rates of noncompliance with licensing and/or have exempted many family day care homes from licensing (based on number of children or on access to public funds). Morgan (1980) argues that these strategies constitute unequal treatment under the law and thus undermine all licensing. Class (1980) suggests that exemptions from licensing based on number of children served actually increases rather than decreases enforcement problems because caregivers feel resent-

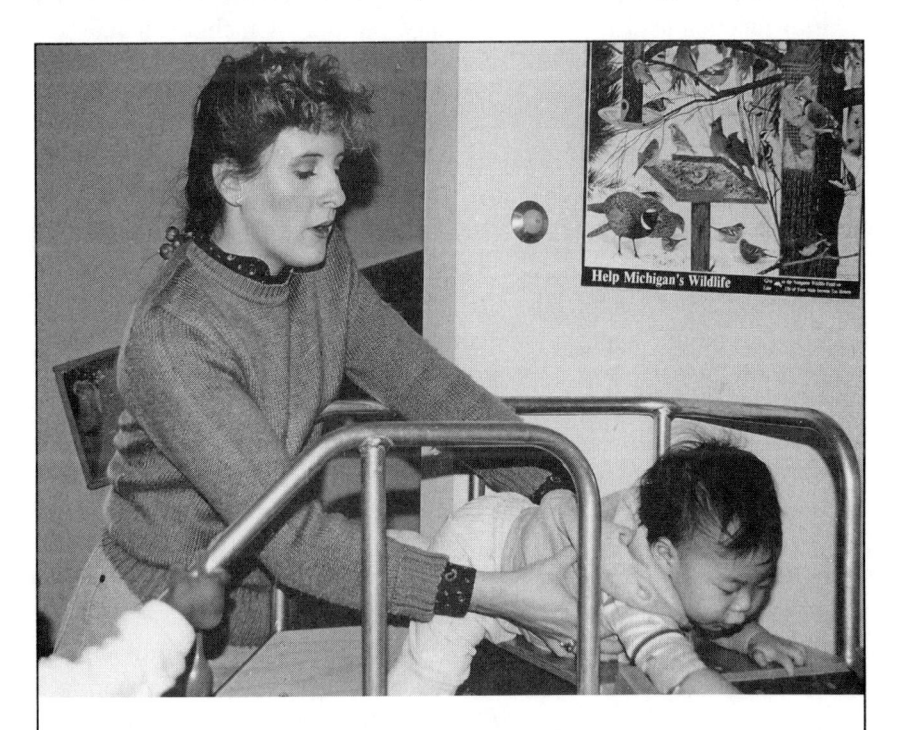

Considering how important caring for and developing children is, it may surprise some readers to learn that 16% of the states do not even have minimum-age requirements for caregivers, and 48% do not have maximum-age requirements. Twenty-five states make no mention of orientation in the regulations, 15 states offer an orientation session in some places, and 11 states require attendance at such a session.

> *Thirty-six states' regulations include space requirements. Most of these states require 35 square feet of indoor space and some outdoor space.*

ment regarding unfairness and unequal treatment. Regulations designed to "ensure protection" that are poorly enforced and adhered to also may provide a false sense of security regarding the safeguards they are maintaining (Morgan, 1980). Both Class and Morgan, as well as the Children's Foundation (1989), take the position that "facility licensure" as applied to child care centers is inappropriate for family day care and should be replaced by a more innovative approach, most likely involving registration.

Beyond these more legalistic and pragmatic reasons for changing the nature of family day care regulations, Morgan (1980) suggests that regulations developed for more institutional services may make it difficult for family day care to function as a real home (as opposed to a "homelike institution"). Morgan also believes that one of the original reasons for licensing—that parents must rely on the state rather than themselves to protect them from inadequate services—is invalid for family day care. According to Morgan, parents are more able to understand and evaluate quality in family day care than in center-based care and thus do not need the protection of the state. As Phillips et al. (1990) pointed out, these assumptions have never been tested and, if accepted at face value, could actually lead to the elimination of family day care regulation completely.

Although no one appears to advocate doing away with family day care regulations, there appears to be a growing consensus that the present system does not work and alternatives need to be found. Change is slow in coming, however. The Children's Foundation (1990) found few new regulatory approaches initiated between 1985 and 1990. The only development worthy of note was that eight states moved from a combination of registration and licensing to using registration only. Suggestions for changes have come from several sources.

The Children's Foundation (1989) recommends that states move toward a flexible registration process and require all family day care providers to become registered. Moreover, the foundation recommends monitoring a random, rotating sample of family day care homes and all homes for which a complaint has been received.

Over 10 years ago, Morgan (1980) laid out several options for improving family day care regulation. One option was to improve the licensing system; for instance, licensing family day care systems ("umbrella" agencies for administering groups of family day care homes) as well as individual family

Twenty-two states have no training requirement! Twenty-nine states require some training, but it may be only in CPR, not necessarily in child development.

day care homes may alleviate some problems. The assumption is that homes that are part of a system do not need to be licensed independently. Another suggestion to improve licensing was to consolidate all family day care requirements across the multitude of jurisdictional authorities into one unified code that is administered by the licensing agency. As a corollary, Morgan recommends that the consolidation process also involve examining each requirement and eliminating any that do not apply to all family residences. A third suggestion was to develop regulatory distinctions between family day care homes and large or group day care homes (typically defined having as 7 to 12 children). The latter, according to Morgan, are more like small, informal centers than family day care homes; thus, a different regulatory approach for them is sensible, assuming it is uniquely suited to the nature and size of the service.

Another regulatory option is to drop licensing in favor of registration. Morgan offers several models of family day care registration that vary in their formality. The most innovative of these models is a credentialing model involving caregiver competencies developed by the state. Caregivers would be eligible for registration following successful completion of a training program designed to develop or nurture these competencies. No state has implemented this model.

A third, more controversial option is deregulation of family day care. According to Morgan, in states without the resources for licensing or the commitment to implement a registration model, this is the only option. She argues that deregulation is not an unthinkable approach because it is "not far from what some states are now doing in practice." For instance, states that only license homes receiving public funds or that exempt homes from licensing based on number of children served (particularly the states that exempt homes with three to five children) are already operating with deregulated family day care for the most part. In states in which it is assumed that parents using family day care neither want nor need state protection, this option may be a viable—not to say desirable—one.

Phillips et al. (1990) make the case that the wide variation in regulatory policies across states and in the number of states with inadequate regulations requires a more active federal role in child care regulation. They recommend, in general, federal-state collaboration to reduce regulatory discrepancies across states and to establish a consistent floor below which quality cannot extend.

More specifically for family day care, they recommend considering "innovative, nonregulatory approaches in conjunction with facility licensing."

Leavitt (1991) makes three recommendations for family day care regulations based on her observations of and interviews with family day care providers. She recommends that caregivers' views be solicited when regulations are created or modified, giving them more ownership of the regulatory process and, it is hoped, reducing compliance and enforcement problems. Also, she recommends that licensing representatives take on the role of consultant. Although the dual role of licensor/consultant might prove to be

One researcher recommends that family day care providers should participate in creating or modifying regulations, giving them more ownership of the regulatory process. It is hoped that this would reduce compliance and enforcement problems.

problematic (Morgan, 1980), there is reason to believe that supervision (perhaps provided by a different agency from the licensing agency) promotes quality in family day care (Corsini, Wisensale, & Caruso, 1988; Rosenthal, 1990). Finally, Leavitt recommends that caregiver self-monitoring be encouraged through systematically establishing and supporting family day care associations. Leavitt's suggestions are designed to recognize and support caregivers in addition to promoting standards.

How do states decide among the options? Morgan (1980) lists three factors that must be considered:

1. the climate of opinion—varying views of the authority of the state to set standards for family day care;

2. the past history of regulation in the state—how active and successful the state has been as a regulator of family day care; and

3. criteria for effectiveness—proportion of caregivers regulated, role of the family, need for inspection, and so forth.

Little research exists that can inform this type of public policy change. One study attempted to compare the relative costs and benefits of licensing versus registration (Harrold, 1976). That study was conducted in a state in which some counties were licensing family day care providers while other counties were registering them. Counties using licensing versus registration were compared regarding the number of homes regulated, the number of rule violations, and the cost of regulation. Results revealed that counties using registration had more regulated homes but also had more rule violations. Either type of registration costs less per regulated home in more heavily populated counties where more homes were regulated. Registration was expected to be less expensive than licensing after the start-up expenses of a public awareness campaign and staff retraining were absorbed.

Fiene and Melnick (1991) compared the use of a self-assessment process regarding child care health and safety features in centers and family day care homes to the traditional assessment conducted by licensing staff. The results of the self-assessment were tied to receipt of technical assistance for caregivers in the areas of greatest need but not to licensing status. Results of the study were promising yet sobering. On the promising side, self-assessment without the threat of punitive action for reporting noncompliance appeared to yield as much or more information about violations of health and safety regulations as

> In the majority of states, family day care homes must operate outside the law because the law regards them as (prohibited) businesses in residential settings.

the traditional assessments conducted by licensing staff. The sobering aspects of these data were the inaccuracy of the traditional assessments and the number of health and safety violations reported by caregivers. The accuracy problems of traditional licensing assessments were attributed to the fact that they are conducted during an announced visit that would result in negative consequences for noncompliance. In addition, licensing staff have nearly double the ideal case load. Under these circumstances, caregivers probably find it easy to fix or cover up areas of noncompliance, and overburdened staff may unintentionally overlook violations. Typical areas of noncompliance reported by family day care providers were fire/evacuation procedures, hot water temperature, and first aid training. This study suggests that self-reports of compliance to family day care regulations could be a useful and cost-effective approach to monitoring if the self-assessment is tied to technical assistance. The results also suggest that, given the serious nature of the licensing violations, technical assistance is certainly warranted.

Another method of obtaining feedback on family day care providers that could be tied to the licensing renewal process was attempted a decade ago in St. Paul, Minnesota (Winget, Winget, & Popplewell, 1982). Parents of children in all licensed family day care homes applying for license renewal were asked to complete a questionnaire regarding their caregiver. Parents rated the frequency of certain caregiver characteristics (e.g., "listened to and talked with child") and facility characteristics (e.g., "safe for child"). In addition, parents rated their satisfaction with specific caregiving practices (e.g., changed diapers as frequently as parent wished). Average ratings across parents were produced for each caregiver, who discussed the ratings with the licensing worker at the time of relicensing. The purpose of the feedback was to "reinforce strengths and correct deficiencies." In general, results revealed that parent feedback was very useful for reinforcing strengths but less useful for correcting deficiencies. The majority of licensing workers (67%) and exactly half of the caregivers believed that parent evaluations should be incorporated into state licensing regulations. The process was deemed to be a "practical and efficient" way to involve parents in child care regulations as well as to increase quality of care and compliance to regulations. More research is needed on approaches to regulation if states are to make informed decisions regarding improved regulatory strategies.

Caregivers' views of regulation

Direct evidence of how caregivers perceive family day care regulation is becoming available. Some of what we know about caregivers' views is obtained indirectly through experts' impressions of caregivers' perceptions of regulation. For instance, Morgan (1980) reported that both parents and caregivers view licensing as an "unwelcome intrusion." According to Morgan, the majority of caregivers neglect to obtain licenses because

1. they are unaware of the laws requiring a license;
2. licensing appears too complicated and expensive;
3. they fear and resent the intrusion of inspections;
4. there is low enforcement and there are no consequences for noncomplance; and
5. parents do not insist on licensing.

Adams (1984) believes that ignorance of state laws and fear or defiance of the law are the primary reasons for noncompliance with licensing regulations. Several studies have examined caregivers' views of licensing.

One of the first studies to focus on caregivers' views of licensing was a survey of 386 licensed family day care home providers in Connecticut (Anderson, 1986). Only 63% of this sample of caregivers reported being aware of the licensing requirement when they originally began caring for children. Those who were not aware of the requirement initially found out about it later through neighbors or friends (29%), another caregiver (28%), the state family day care licensing agency (24%), or the newspaper (16%). When asked why they chose to become licensed, their responses varied. The sample was split between those caregivers who said the legal requirement played a part in their decision (42%) and those who said it was not a factor (40%). Other reasons for becoming licensed included the possibility of receiving information about health and safety or program planning and activities (60%), being reviewed and receiving feedback from trained individuals (53%), obtaining help with recruiting children (44%), and the potential of joining a family day care association (40%). For these caregivers, it appears that a sense of professionalism and/or a need for a support network were major factors in obtaining licensing. In states in which licensing does not give a caregiver access to referrals, feedback, or networking opportunities, caregivers might respond differently.

Anderson (1986) asked the licensed caregivers in her sample to speculate as to why many caregivers choose not to become licensed. The caregivers cited two major factors. The majority (more than 60%) responded that economic factors were major disincentives for licensing—more specifically, unwillingness to limit the number of children served or to list family day care income on their income tax returns. Over one-half of the licensed caregivers said that the other major factor resulting in noncompliance was concern about privacy or unwillingness to allow into their homes state licensing officials who would perhaps even tell them what to do. Few caregivers (10%) believed that noncompliance results from a perception that licensing is expensive. These data are consistent with the Morgan (1980) and Adams (1984) accounts of caregivers' reluctance to become licensed.

Leavitt (1991) interviewed a small group of Illinois licensed family day care providers regarding their views of the licensing process. She found that the caregivers most strongly objected to regulations regarding group size and composition. By and large, these caregivers believed that they should regulate themselves on these two standards because they, better than the state, know their ability to handle a particular number or age range of children; thus, some caregivers knowingly violate state standards restricting group size and composition. Several more practical issues, however, seem to be behind some of the objections to outside regulation in this area. Some caregivers reportedly rely on other caregivers to cover for them when they must run errands, visit the doctor, and so forth, during the day. When one caregiver is in charge of two groups of children, licensing standards usually are compromised. Another concern expressed by caregivers is the income restrictions placed on them by group size and composition regulations. Some caregivers believe that in order to charge parents affordable fees and still earn an adequate income, they must care for more children or more infants and toddlers than the regulations allow.

It is important to point out that these caregivers did not disagree with the intent of licensing regulations to protect children from harmful conditions of care. They simply believed that rigid standards regarding group size and composition are unnecessary and unrealistic and that licensing standards, in general, are idealistic. For several caregivers, this idealism was symbolized by the prohibition of corporal punishment. They believed that spanking is a "natural" response to reaching one's limits and is necessary to keep the children's behavior under control. Leavitt (1991) makes the point that these caregivers' views on licensing standards reveal very limited understanding of the relationship between quality of care and such regulated variables as group size and composition, discipline, and the like. This limited understanding, combined with the practical dilemmas of regulatory compliance confronting caregivers on a daily basis, makes licensing regulations seem arbitrary and unrealistic.

Although these studies of licensed family day care providers' views of regulation and licensing are revealing and their impressions of unlicensed caregivers' views are of interest, to gain an accurate understanding of

Some family day care providers choose to become licensed because they believe it will help them recruit children, get expert feedback, and network. Others avoid licensing because they fear that the authorities will limit the number of children they are allowed to have and because they do not want to report this income to the IRS. Some providers resent the possibility that someone will "monitor" their home.

The vast majority of states prohibit physical punishment.

unlicensed caregivers' views on these issues we must ask them directly. Several studies did just that. Nelson (1991b) administered questionnaires to 225 registered Vermont family day care providers (49% of the total population of caregivers in the state) and 110 unregistered family day care providers. The unregistered caregivers were located via advertising in local newspapers, referral by community members, and referral by other caregivers. In addition to the complete questionnaires, 40 unregistered caregivers and 30 registered caregivers were interviewed.

The questionnaire asked unregistered caregivers to indicate why they were not registered. In this group, ignorance of the law and reluctance to incur the expense of registration were given by very few people as reasons for failure to register. Only three percent had never heard of registration or licensing, and only eight percent indicated that the expense of registration was a reason. Although more of the unregistered caregivers (17%) reported that they did not know the procedures for becoming registered, very few (4%) said this was the most important reason for not registering. There were also few caregivers (3%) who were unregistered because they were not in compliance for group size or because they were reluctant to reduce income by reducing group size.

A sizable minority of unregistered caregivers (25%) believed that states should not regulate day care in private homes, and 18% indicated that this was their primary reason for not being registered. Interestingly, 52% of the unregistered caregivers agreed with the statement, "As long as child care is offered in a private home, the government should not be involved." More than one-third of the caregivers (35%) believed that registration has no benefits, and 19% gave this as their reason for not doing so. The most common reason given for failure to register, however, was belief that their situation was exempt from regulation (51%). These data are not consistent with previous impressions gleaned from experts or from licensed caregivers. Although the results are based on just one sample in one state, their strength lies in the fact that, unlike the caregiving sampled in earlier reports, unregulated caregivers were the source of information.

Nelson (1991b) also attempted to assess caregivers' knowledge of registration standards. The rule for registration in Vermont at the time the study was conducted was that any caregiver serving more than two different *families* is required to register regardless of the number of children in care. Only 52% of the unregistered caregivers were aware of this rule. Many caregivers justified

What should be done to improve the regulatory process?

their failure to register based on the number of children or the amount of care they provided.

Once a caregiver is registered in Vermont, the regulations permit six full-time preschool children (including a maximum of two infants) and four part-time school-age children. Fewer than one-half of the unregistered caregivers (46%) could accurately report the number of full-time children allowed, and the rest were split between those who over- and underestimated the number. Just over one-third of the unregistered caregivers (37%) could accurately report the maximum number of children allowed. The remaining caregivers believed that the maximum number was smaller than it actually is; none overestimated this number. Finally, fewer than one-half of the unregistered caregivers (44%) knew that the total number of children in care must include the caregiver's own children. These data document substantial gaps in the knowledge of unregistered caregivers regarding state family day care standards.

Not only were caregivers poorly informed about standards, they were also misinformed about what the registration process involved. The most noticeable misinformation was the inaccurate belief that registration required an inspection of the water supply (56%) and that a fenced outside play area was required (56%), both potentially problematic items for a largely rural sample of caregivers. A sizable minority of unregistered caregivers also inaccurately believed that registration required annual training (27%) and a medical exam for themselves (25%) and allowed spanking of children with parents' permission (24%). According to Nelson (1991b), less than one-half of the unregistered caregivers could accurately respond to more than two-thirds of the questions about regulation. For these caregivers, knowledge of family day care standards as well as the process of registration were both lacking.

Are caregivers who are ignorant of family day care standards also out of compliance with them as a result? Based on caregiver self-report, Nelson (1991b) found that the unregistered family day care providers were typically in compliance with respect to group size and composition (although 13% of the caregivers reported out-of-compliance group sizes at lunchtime). In addition, 77% to 86% of the caregivers reported meeting certain equipment standards by having a smoke detector on each floor, a heating system inspection within the last year, a fire extinguisher, and a first-aid kit, These figures are important in light of the results of a 1986 random inspection of registered family day care providers in Vermont that found that 15% cared for

Many questions are being raised about the state of family day care regulation. In response, suggestions for improvement of current regulatory systems are being put forth. Although no one has yet proposed a solution (perhaps the Children's Foundation, 1989 comes the closest to this aim), at the heart of the discussion is whether licensing is the appropriate regulatory approach for family day care, particularly if the goal is universal compliance with family day care regulations. Also of concern are effectiveness of various types of registration systems and the desirability of federal involvement in child care regulation in general, but family day care regulation in particular. Research with family day care providers themselves suggests that there is dissatisfaction with current regulatory approaches. There is also considerable misinformation on the part of unregulated caregivers. There seems to be some resistance on the part of caregivers to the notion of state regulation of a service occurring in a private home.

Monitor only a rotating sample of day care homes and all homes for which a complaint has been received?

too many children; 21% did not have a tested, functioning smoke detector; and 57% did not have an adequate fire extinguisher (Vermont, 1986, cited in Nelson, 1991b). These data indicate that unregistered family day care providers were neither invariably out of compliance with the regulations nor invariably in compliance. In fact, if caregiver self-reports are at all reliable indicators, the rates of noncompliance for registered and unregistered caregivers may be remarkably similar. This is not necessarily an argument for deregulation. More likely it is a reflection of the fact that unregulated caregivers typically serve fewer children for fewer hours per week and are less businesslike in their work than are regulated caregivers (e.g., Divine-Hawkins, 1981; Fischer, 1989; Nelson, 1991b [see Chapter 2]).

In another study of unregulated and "reluctantly regulated" family day care providers, caregivers considered regulation to be an intrusion that reduced their autonomy (Enarson, 1991). They also complained of "harassment" by regulators. Caregivers did not deny the need for quality control; they simply believed that this function lay in the hands of parents and themselves, not the government. Licensing was viewed as another step closer to child care as businesslike and professional rather than as a "labor of love" and akin to mothering. Similar attitudes were reflected in Zinsser's (1990) discussions with family day care providers who limited their group sizes to stay legally unlicensed and failed to report their income to the Internal Revenue Service.

Summary

Many questions are being raised about the state of family day care regulation. In response, suggestions for improvement of current regulatory systems are being put forth. Although no one has yet proposed a solution (perhaps the Children's Foundation, 1989, comes the closest to this aim), at the heart of the discussion is whether licensing is the appropriate regulatory approach for family day care, particularly if the goal is universal compliance with family day care regulations (Class, 1980; Morgan, 1980; Children's Foundation, 1989). Also of concern are the effectiveness of various types of registration systems (Morgan, 1980; Children's Foundation, 1989) and the desirability of federal involvement in child care regulation in general, but family day care regulation in particular (Phillips, Lande, & Goldberg, 1990).

License family day care systems, *not every home that is part of the system?*

Research with family day care providers themselves suggests that there is dissatisfaction with current regulatory approaches (Enarson, 1991; Leavitt, 1991) and considerable misinformation on the part of unregulated caregivers (Nelson, 1991b). There seems to be some resistance on the part of caregivers to the notion of state regulation of a service occurring in a private home (Anderson, 1986; Enarson, 1991; Nelson, 1991b).

Accreditation

Another approach to regulating program quality is accreditation. Different from governmental regulations, which are designed to designate the "floor" of quality below which no program is allowed to go and for which compliance is mandated, accreditation involves standards set within the field—usually by a professional organization—with which compliance is optional (Morgan, 1985). Moreover, accreditation standards are designed to designate, not minimal standards, but the "ceiling" of quality or criteria for optimal early childhood programming. For family day care providers, two types of accreditation are available that each result in a nationally recognized credential. Although there are some other family day care accreditation programs in place across the country (e.g., Child Care Partnership of Dallas, Louise Child Care [see Modigliani, no date]), because they are only available locally at this time, they will not be discussed here. The two nationally recognized accreditation programs are administered by the Council for Early Childhood Professional Recognition (the Child Development Associate National Credentialing Program, or CDA) and the National Association for Family Day Care (NAFDC). These two programs will first be described; then their advantages and disadvantages will be compared and their impact (real and potential) assessed.

CDA Family Day Care credential

To earn a CDA credential, a family day care provider must meet eligibility requirements. A caregiver must be 18 years old, care for at least two children unrelated to her who are under age six, have 10 months' experience in family day care and 640 hours of experience with children under age six, comply with

Develop regulatory distinctions between family day care homes and large or group homes that are more like informal centers?

local/state regulations, be literate, and have had at least three relevant educational experiences of some type (formal or informal; two of them must be specific to early childhood education/child development). Under new eligibility rules taking effect in 1992, caregivers will also be required to have a high school diploma or a GED, 120 hours of formal training, and 480 hours of experience with preschool children.

The CDA program has set competency standards for family day care in 13 functional areas:

1. safe,
2. healthy,
3. learning environment,
4. physical,
5. cognitive,
6. communication,
7. creative,
8. self,
9. social,
10. guidance,
11. families,
12. program management, and
13. professionalism.

For each functional area, a developmental context is provided for all ages and for four different age levels: young infants (birth to 9 months), mobile infants (6 to 18 months), toddlers (16 to 36 months), and preschoolers (3- to 5-year-olds). In addition, examples of competent caregiver behavior for each functional area are given, specific to each age level.

Beginning in 1992 (effective for all family day care providers who apply for CDA credentialing after September 1, 1991), there will be two procedures for obtaining a CDA family day care credential: "Direct Assessment" and the "Professional Preparation Program." Direct Assessment involves a procedure similar to the original CDA credentialing process. Caregivers may determine their own 120 hours of formal training, but it must take place in organized, ongoing programs rather than in conferences or one-time workshops. In

Or something else? There are also other options,

addition, the formal training must be distributed across designated competency areas. Caregivers must choose a Local Advisory Team (LAT) consisting of an advisor and a parent/community representative. The LAT gathers information by observing the candidate and obtaining questionnaires from parents of enrolled children. The purpose of the information gathering is to determine to what extent the candidate meets the competency standards specified by the credentialing organization. To supplement this information, a national CDA representative observes and interviews the candidate and meets with the team. The candidate also must take an objective test on the competency standards. Depending on positive test results and the recommendation of the LAT meeting with the CDA representative, the national office awards the credential. If the test is not passed or the committee does not approve a credential, further training may be recommended.

The Professional Preparation Program is a procedure that more closely resembles traditional methods of formal training. It is a one-year training program for both center- and home-based caregivers. Candidates begin the program by working in a child care setting, meeting weekly with their advisors, and completing assignments. Midway through the program, candidates enroll in 120 hours of college seminars. At the end, candidates are observed working in a family day care home and meet with a CDA representative for an oral assessment. Successful completion of this sequence results in awarding of the credential.

Regardless of which procedure a family day care provider chooses for working toward a credential, the fee is $325 until May 31, 1992, and $650 thereafter. The credential must be renewed in three years; a renewal is valid for five years. Candidates may work toward the credential for 12 weeks to one year or more. To date, 521 family day care providers nationwide have received a CDA credential.

NAFDC accreditation

To be eligible for accreditation by NAFDC, a family day care provider must have provided care for the previous 18 months and meet all state family day care regulations (voluntary and mandatory). Each caregiver selects a parent validator who does not currently have a child in her care. A training program

In one study, approximately one-half of the unregistered caregivers asked agreed with the statement, "As long as child care is offered in a private home, the government should not be involved."

is not required, but Modigliani (no date) reported that most caregivers need some sort of support (to prepare their homes and programs to meet accreditation standards) to successfully complete the process. Caregivers may select a colleague or other knowledgeable person for support and assistance. The caregiver then completes a self-assessment profile, using the Assessment Profile for Family Day Care (Sibley & Abbott-Shim, 1987). A Study Guide (Sibley & Abbott-Shim, 1989) for the Assessment Profile is available from NAFDC to help caregivers prepare for the assessment. Parents with a child enrolled in the caregiver's program must complete a survey. Then the parent validator and a NAFDC validator observe the family day care home for a minimum of six hours and complete the Assessment Profile. All materials are submitted to NAFDC for scoring and returned to the caregiver, who must then review the evaluation results and write an accreditation report to be submitted to NAFDC. To be awarded accreditation, a caregiver's scores must average 85% across all the dimensions and not go below 75% on any dimension by any observer. In addition to the scores on the Assessment Profile, the caregiver's written report and parent survey determine whether or not she is accredited.

The Assessment Profile for Family Day Care is a structured observation guide for evaluating a family day care home in terms of its physical characteristics, child care procedures and policies, and adult/child interactions. Specifically, seven dimensions of child care are assessed:

1. indoor safety,
2. health,
3. nutrition,
4. interacting,
5. indoor play environment,
6. outdoor play environment, and
7. professional responsibility.

The profile consists of 171 general items and an additional 18 items specific to caregivers responsible for infants. Each item is scored *yes* or *no*, and the score is based on the proportion of *yeses* for each of the dimensions.

The fee for NAFDC accreditation is $150 for members of the organization ($250 for nonmembers), payable in two installments of $75 (initially at the time of application and then when the completed evaluation materials are

> *More than one-third of the unregistered caregivers in this study believed that registration brings no benefits.*

submitted). Applicants have 60 days to complete the accreditation process. Accreditation is valid for three years and is updated annually. The update involves a self-assessment—using the Assessment Profile—and submission of a professional development resume. Currently, 122 family day care providers have been awarded a Certificate of Accreditation from NAFDC.

Comparison of accreditation programs

Among the more obvious differences between the two accreditation processes are the cost and the time involved. The CDA credential is more costly (although some scholarships are available for income-eligible caregivers) and takes longer to earn. NAFDC accreditation ties family day care providers to a professional organization, while the CDA credential does not. Some of the other differences are more subtle.

In a systematic comparison of five instruments used to assess family child care quality, including the CDA and NAFDC instruments, Modigliani (no date) concluded that the CDA assessment provides the most comprehensive set of criteria for quality in family day care, including an explanation of the underlying rationale of the instrument and differentiation by ages of children in care. The comprehensiveness of the criteria, however, is counterbalanced by their vagueness and difficulty of interpretation. The NAFDC instrument, on the other hand, provides very specific criteria for quality that are clear and less open to interpretation, but the assessment is less comprehensive. Modigliani points out that there is limited measure of caregivers' play facilitation skills, skills unique to caring for infants and toddlers, relations with families, and multicultural approaches to curriculum planning.

Both accreditation programs award the credential to caregivers who are providing moderate- and high-quality care (Modigliani, no date). In other words, no special distinctions are made for family day care providers performing exceptionally well. One reason for this approach in the CDA program may be that there is a priority on flexibility, acknowledgment of individual differences, and acceptance of multiple indicators of a competency (Modigliani, no date). These priorities might be hard to maintain if finer distinctions were being made in the competence of family day care providers. NAFDC sets a minimum score to qualify for accreditation but weights equally items that are not of equal importance. Consequently, a caregiver can become accredited without demonstrating some critical skills (Modigliani, no date).

NAFDC accreditation is easier to achieve for family child care providers who do not have access to training or assistance. Providers who have access to training and/or assistance will probably go through the process more easily, but neither is a requirement. This is not true for a CDA credential. Family day care providers are required to have access to training and assistance in order to be eligible for the program. In some areas, this requirement could make the CDA credential an unreachable goal.

Both accreditation programs offer nationally recognized credentials that give professional recognition to family day care providers. Both programs

It is hoped that professional recognition will boost providers' self-esteem and help parents choose better care for their children. Motivation for pursuing accreditation may be primarily intrinsic: a desire for a sense of professionalism, pride in one's work, and opportunities to socialize and network with colleagues.

Other data document substantial gaps in the knowledge of unregistered caregivers regarding their state's family day care standards.

recognize caregivers providing moderate- to high-quality care. Each program has its strengths and weaknesses, as previously enumerated. Consequently, it is meaningless to pronounce one as superior to the other. Selection of an accreditation program must be based on the needs of the family day care provider and the resources available to her.

Whether either of these accreditation programs offers anything resembling what might be considered ideal (given the boundaries of practicality) is an issue that needs to be addressed if family day care accreditation is the wave of the future. Modigliani (no date) identifies some important issues regarding what accreditation means and the form it should take. For instance, what high-quality family day care looks like and whether it can be "educational" in the same sense as either a family or a child care center are issues that need to be addressed. Other issues are how high standards should be and whether criteria should be general or specific. The value of recognizing more than one level of quality needs to be explored, as does the link between training and accreditation. More controversial, perhaps, are the issues of whether there should be one nationally recognized form of accreditation and whether accreditation should be tied to regulation in any way. Seeking a consensus in the field on these complex issues should lead us to an understanding of what the accreditation process ought to be.

Impact of accreditation

Based on the number of caregivers who have successfully completed the accreditation process, the impact of these two programs can be said to be quite small. Both programs are so new, however, that judging their impact solely on numbers is unfair. Modigliani (no date) argues that the accreditation process has a number of benefits. One very important benefit is the identification of standards of quality that are higher than "floor of quality" state standards. By giving professional recognition to deserving family day care providers, it is hoped that accreditation will raise their self-esteem. The availability of accreditation, according to Modigliani, offers incentives to caregivers to improve their skills and may draw them into training experiences they might not otherwise seek. Finally, accreditation helps parents identify quality family day care. Parents who are aware of the process and its significance may seek

To date, 521 family day care providers nationwide have earned a CDA credential, and 122 have earned a Certificate of Accreditation from NAFDC.

accredited caregivers. Although several of these benefits are obviously true, others are only assumptions or wishful thinking at this time. No studies have been conducted to objectively examine the outcomes of accreditation, particularly its impact on caregivers' self-esteem and child care skills, and on parents' search for quality family day care. As greater numbers of caregivers seek and achieve accreditation, studies of this type will become a priority.

One qualitative study has been conducted on the impact of accreditation (Cohen & Modigliani, 1990). An informal evaluation was conducted of the impact on quality of a family day care training and accreditation program at four sites funded by Mervyn's Family-to-Family Project. Two staff members at each site were interviewed regarding how many and who were seeking accreditation and their motives for doing so, obstacles to accreditation and recommendations to overcome them, and accreditation's influence on quality of care. The interviewees had not engaged in a formal data collection process but responded to questions based on their impressions gathered as they worked with the family day care providers.

The interviewees at all four sites were optimistic regarding the number of family day care providers seeking accreditation, although they recognized that initiating these types of activities takes time when few or no professional development opportunities have been available to caregivers in the past. Three of the sites reported that caregivers seeking accreditation were likely to be young, White, middle-income mothers. In one community, those most likely to seek accreditation were mothers (of grown children) who had acquired more time for extracurricular activities. Motivation for pursuing accreditation was primarily intrinsic: a desire for a sense of professionalism, pride in one's work, and opportunities to socialize and network with colleagues. Extrinsic motivations such as increased pay and status were not expected, nor did these potential benefits materialize. The interviewees expressed concern that for caregivers without the intrinsic motivation, accreditation was unlikely to be attractive.

The biggest obstacles to accreditation were cost and time. These obstacles might be minimized, according to the respondents, if the cost were subsidized and if extrinsic rewards followed accreditation. Respondents were convinced that accreditation led to higher quality family day care and helped caregivers

Here is a comparison of the two accreditation systems. Each has its advantages, but both offer nationally recognized credentials that give professional recognition to family day care providers.

"translate training into practice." They also believed that accreditation led to higher self-confidence among caregivers.

To promote the accreditation process in the future, interviewees identified four strategies:

1. Assign mentors to caregivers.

2. Conduct home visits to help caregivers meet accreditation standards.

3. Integrate accreditation into training.

4. Organize recognition activities (media attention, ceremonies, letters to clients, and so forth).

The respondents seemed to believe that NAFDC accreditation was more realistic to start with and that CDA represented another step toward higher quality. Both programs were viewed as viable options with different strengths and weaknesses.

Summary

Accreditation represents the "carrot" approach to achieving quality family day care in contrast to the "stick" approach of regulation. Two types of nationally recognized accreditation are available to family day care providers: CDA and NAFDC. A CDA credential costs more and takes more time to earn than NAFDC accreditation but has more comprehensive criteria for quality family day care. NAFDC accreditation is more feasible for caregivers without access to training or support. At this time, relatively few caregivers have become accredited through either CDA or NAFDC because both programs are relatively new.

No hard evidence is available regarding the impact of accreditation on family day care. To demonstrate that accreditation (via CDA or NAFDC) results in higher quality family day care and entices caregivers into training, documentation of improved caregiving practices and increased training following accreditation is needed. In addition, accredited caregivers should compare favorably to a comparable group of caregivers who are not accredited. Finally, strategies for motivating family day care providers to seek training and accreditation must be investigated.

Chapter 7

Training

TRAINING, PRESERVICE AND IN-SERVICE, is at the heart of discussions about quality child care. Many people would say that a child care environment is only as good as the caregivers working in it. Because in family day care homes the caregiver is usually the sole adult in charge, her influence is even more pervasive than is the influence of caregivers in center-based settings who invariably have colleagues who also work with the children. Thus, the qualifications that a caregiver brings to her work are important considerations.

We know from our examination of the characteristics of family child care providers in Chapter 2 that the typical caregiver has a high school diploma and little or no formal training in child care or child development. Perhaps even more important, we also know that caregivers frequently (although not universally) view their mothering experiences as adequate preparation for being involved in family day care, and a substantial number have no desire for training. Complicating this factor is the perception of some caregivers, perhaps unlicensed caregivers in particular, that they are babysitters rather than child care workers and thus, by definition, are untrained (Zinsser, 1990). How does one effectively provide training for a group with little incentive to seek it, who may not perceive a need for it, or who may even perceive training as an inappropriate attempt to transform caregivers from "nurturers" to "teachers"? Further complicating matters are high job turnover among family day care providers as well as the fact that so many family day care providers are unlicensed and, for all practical purposes, out of contact with typical sources of training.

To answer the question of how to effectively provide training under these circumstances, we will examine the literature on past or existing training programs in family day care. The goal is, through analysis of successful components of these programs, to draw conclusions about what effective training for family day care providers is.

Training, preservice and in-service, is at the heart of discussions about quality child care. Many people would say that a child care environment is only as good as the caregivers working in it. Because in family day care homes the caregiver is usually the sole adult in charge, her influence is even more pervasive than that of caregivers in center-based settings who invariably have colleagues who also work with the children. Thus, the qualifications that a caregiver brings to her work are important considerations. Of the training programs included in this review, the majority conducted training via group sessions (workshops, "rap" groups, and so forth) combined with home visiting. It was less common to conduct just group sessions or home visits, and it was rare to do neither. Only three programs (Colbert & Enos, 1976; Greenspan et al., 1977; Poresky, 1977) included group sessions but no home visits, and three (Rubin, 1974; Howes, 1988; Machida, 1990) included home visits but no group sessions.

Looking at successful components of training programs

There are many fine examples of family day care training programs across the country in local and regional agencies. The programs included in this chapter's analysis, however, consist of programs that have been published in monographs, journals, or accessible data bases; only 20 programs met that criterion. Two additional unpublished programs were included—because of their evaluation component—for a total of 22 programs. A premium was placed on reports that included program evaluation data, particularly those that used a control or comparison group to contrast with the trained family day care providers. Fifteen of the programs included an evaluation component, but very few (five) involved a control or comparison group.

Of the 20 published programs, 11 (55%) were reported in the 1970s, while the remaining programs were reported between 1982 and 1990. The reports from the 1970s were more likely to have been written by or about programs located in community agencies, while the more recent reports were more likely to be written and conducted by university personnel. A summary of each of the 22 programs is included in the table on page 122. The format, length, and content of training are listed for each program as are the outcome measures and results of the evaluation. The balance of this chapter will be devoted to an analysis of the format, content, intensity, and outcomes of the family day care training programs included in the table. Correlates of and barriers to training will also be discussed.

Training format

Of the training programs included in this review, the majority conducted training via group sessions (workshops, "rap" groups, and so forth) combined with home visiting. It was less common to conduct just group sessions or home visits, and it was rare to do neither. Only three programs (Colbert & Enos, 1976; Greenspan et al., 1977; Poresky, 1977) included group sessions but no home visits, and three (Rubin, 1974; Howes, Keeling, & Sale, 1988; Machida, 1990) included home visits but no group sessions. Only one program (Marshall, 1987), a home-study course, included neither.

Table. Summary of Family Day Care Training Programs

Author/ Year/State	Format	Length	Content	Outcomes	Results
Radin/1970/MI	Home visits Group discussions	Bimonthly (9 months) Six (3 months)	Varied/individualized	Childrearing attitudes and child management strategies Locus of control Professionalism Children's development Subjective reaction	No difference between experimental and control groups in childrearing attitudes or child management strategies, locus of control, or children's development. Experimental group members were more likely to reject the homemaker role. Caregivers believed the project was more worthwhile and enjoyed it.
Rausch & Crowell/ 1974/HI	Preservice —workshops —practicum In-service —rap groups —workshops —home visitor with toys/equipment and ideas for use	4 to 5 weeks —2 days/ week —2 days/ week Weekly Bimonthly	Health/nutrition/safety, infant care, growth and development, relating to parents, stimulation programs	Child development and child care skills and knowledge Quality of caregiver/child interaction	Ratings of children's language development showed that the children were making developmental gains. There was a correlation between quality of caregiver/child interaction and children's communication and interaction skills. Test of knowledge and skills showed general improvement.
Rubin/1974, 1975/ MA	Home visits (family day care system)	Monthly (ongoing)	Varied/individualized	Attitudes of providers and visitors regarding each	Providers valued the role of the visitor but saw their role as primarily interacting with children

				other's ideal and actual behavior	and secondarily with the visitor. Providers wanted visitors to relieve them from caregiving duties; they received less feedback from visitors than they would have liked. Visitors saw their role as support, not training. Considerable variation existed in content/format of visits.
Pine/1975; Crowe, Pine, & Titus/1977/NY	Varied —resources —resource center —workshops —8-week certificate course —newsletter —equipment-lending library (Cornell Cooperative Extension Services)	Ongoing (3 years)	Varied; generated by family day care participants	Activities provided Number of people involved Knowledge, attitude, skill change Practice change (self-report)	105 family day care providers completed the certificate course. The certificate course resulted in a significant increase in knowledge of child development and child care practice. County Family Day Care Mothers Association was formed. 177 family day care providers (120 licensed) were involved in the program. Self-reports of child care skills and attitudes were unrelated to the level of program participation. No difference in child care skills and attitudes between participants and comparison group on 9 out of 10 items. No evidence of changes in self-esteem or job attitudes. Weak evidence of change in practices.
Colbert & Enos/1976/IL	Workshops Newsletter Toy- and book-lending library	11 biweekly for 3 hours Monthly for 4 months Biweekly	Workshops: child development, parents, role of caregiver, taxes, making teaching materials, children's art	Personal and occupational self-concept Knowledge of child development Attitudes toward childrearing	No diffrence between pre- and posttest of self-concept. Decrease in number of caregivers who described themselves as babysitters. Knowledge of child development test scores increased from 7.6 to 9.6 (out of a maximum of 13).

Author/ Year/State	Format	Length	Content	Outcomes	Results
Brout & Krabbenhoft/1977/NY	Workshops Rap sessions Option for college credit Home visits from paraprofessionals	4 weeks 7-1/2 hours per week	Newsletter: tips for activities, field trips, recipes, childrearing Health, nutrition, budgeting, discipline, learning through play Support, counseling, community information	Behavior change (observations) Sense of professionalism Enriching environment for children	No change between pre- and posttest on childrearing attitudes. Postobservations revealed more playing with children and verbal teaching and questioning. Case study documenting desired outcomes.
Greenspan et al./1977/MD	Group "therapy" sessions	Seven 1-1/2 hour sessions	Psychodynamically oriented sessions focusing on family day care responsibilities, "bad" parents, "problem" children, separation Goal of developing caregiver empathy toward children to facilitate emotional development	Group leaders and caregiver ratings of improved performance Projective test	Subjective ratings of improvement from both leaders and caregivers (fewer problem children, new ways to help, etc.). Projective posttest rated better than pretest for 43% of items.

Poresky/1977/ KS	8 to 11 workshops —professional staff trained family day care providers who trained other family day care providers (Wichita Child Day Care Assn.)	6 months	Sketchy information provided, e.g., activities for children, meal planning	Child care knowledge and skill, job satisfaction, child care attitudes, self-concepts	Some change in knowledge and self-reports of skill by family day care trainers, but not by trainees. No changes in self-concept or attitudes.
Wattenberg/ 1977/MN	University course work on TV/radio or formal classes Vo/tech courses or training seminars Workshops Field trips with training packets Home-based training	Varied by format	Varied	Characteristics of high versus low users	Variables that differentiated high and low users —possession of driver's license —experience in family day care —continuity of experience —number of children in care —previous occupation —use of toy resource center (traditional versus modernized).
Goldsmith/1979/ RI	Neighborhood —discussion groups/workshops Television —television series for family day care, providers accompanied by a discussion group	3 times per week; then monthly for rest of year 10 parts	Discipline, child development, health, first aid and nutrition, planning activities etc. No mention	Increase awareness of the importance of family day care Increase knowledge of day care procedures Upgrade quality of day care Change attitudes toward family day care	Caregivers expressed a lessened sense of isolation and a new awareness of the importance of their work; improved sense of self-worth reported. No mention.

Author/ Year/State	Format	Length	Content	Outcomes	Results
	College —work/study paraprofessional program to become family day care home consultants; included coursework and home visits to caregivers	2 years/tuition fee/ stipend	Coursework: child development and management skills, creative activities, communication skills Field work: establish 4 neighborhood resource centers and conduct home visits	Stimulate changes in behavior toward children and parents Career ladder Direct support services to caregivers	Consultant/trainees reported skill gains, especially in established rapport with family day care providers. 61.9% of caregivers believed home visits were "very helpful." 77.9% of caregivers believed group discussions were "very helpful." 98% of caregivers believed the program was beneficial and should be continued.
Kilmer/1979/MN	Individual training visits 1 group meeting	5 to 6 meetings of 1-1/2 to 2 hours	Individually chosen, but usually included parent-provider relations, recruiting children, contacts and fees, guidance, activeties, and taxes and business	Caregiver reports of satisfaction and behavior change	75% of caregivers reported that training changed their behavior. 90% reported that the training was useful and would recommend it to a friend.
Kaplan & Smock/ 1982/MI	Formal class with discussion and outside speakers	20 hours minimum	Selected from 15 competencies	Child care philosophy and information Behavior	Child care information score higher for experimental group than for control group. One-third of behaviors showed significant improvement posttraining (N=9).
Jones & Meisels/ 1987/MI	Workshops Home visits Toy- and resource-lending library	13 bimonthly for 1 year	Caring for children with special needs Knowledge about child development and planning appropriate activities Adult-child interaction	Attitudes toward disabled children Knowledge about working with disabled children Overall child care quality (FDCRS)	No change in attitudes. Increased knowledge about caring for special-needs children. Improved child care quality.

Marshall/1987/TX	In-home study—videotapes and manual (extension services)	4 weeks	Health and safety, business, nutrition, child development and guidance	Practice changes (self-report) New knowledge (test) Helpfulness ratings	72% were changing *some* practice. Knowledge test scores increased from 55% to 68% (on the average). 87% to 99% rated aspects of the program "helpful" to "very helpful."
Ungaretti/1987/MD	Experimental group—college course (6 credits) Control group—informal discussion groups	Weekly meetings for 3 months Every 3 weeks for 3 months	Child development Multiage activities Health, safety, and nutrition Business practices "Spoonful of Lovin'"	Overall child care quality	FDCRS posttest total score was significantly greater for the experimental group than for the control group.
Deiner & Whitehead/1988/DE	General workshop training Specific training Home visits Newsletter Toy-lending library	16 hours 6 hours Bimonthly Bimonthly	Normal/atypical development, teaching disabled infants/toddlers, supporting families, using community resources, getting support Special needs of disabled child placed by the project	Ability to provide respite care services to families of disabled children	Case study documenting how respite care in family day care can meet child *and* family needs.
Howes, Keeling, & Sale/1988/CA	Home visits; or Toy loan (resource and referral agency)	2 visits per 3 months; or 4 visits per 3 months, bimonthly	Child development and health concerns	Overall child care quality (FDCRS subscales and total score)	Home visiting, regardless of frequency, resulted in significant FDCRS score increases.

Author/ Year/State	Format	Length	Content	Outcomes	Results
Kontos/1988b/IN	Workshops Home visits Toy- and resource-lending library	6 sessions, each 3-1/2 hours Weekly	Special needs, quality child care, program planning, teaching strategies, behavior management, working with parents Individualized yearly training objectives determined content	Early intervention skills (self-report) Overall child care quality Social validity (by key participants)	Providers decreased the number of skills needed "to learn" or "with assistance" from 68% to 8.8%. FDCRS total scores increased from 114 to 166 (out of 231). Caregivers unanimously agreed that workshops, visits, and lending libraries were good preparation for intervention. Parents were positive but did not view family day care as early intervention. Special educators were skeptical about skills of family day care providers.
Vartuli/1989/KS	Group meetings Home visits Radio broadcasts Resource- and toy-lending library	Monthly 2-hour meeting Monthly Twenty-six 15-minute scripts over 9 months	CDA competencies for family day care	Usefulness of meetings and home visits Child development knowledge and attitudes Behavior change	More than 90% of caregivers rated the meetings and visits as useful. Knowledge and attitudes increased from pre- to post-training. Observations of trained caregivers and a control group revealed no differences in behavior.
Lawrence, Brown, & Bellin/1989/CA	College classes Topical workshops Telephone advice lines Home visits Toy- and resource-lending library	No information	Business practices	Retention	Of 168 caregivers contacted (out of 217), 109 were active caregivers after one year.
Machida/1990/CA	Home visits with handouts, charts, etc.	3 visits (1 for evaluation purposes)	Individualized; covered 10 topics per visit related to health/safety issues (e.g., infections, childhood diseases, skin problems, first aid and safety, etc.)	Child health knowledge and practice (questionnaire, interview, observation) Satisfaction	After training, caregivers scored 76% correct on the questionnaire (minimal knowledge). No relation between number of topics covered and knowledge, but knowledge was related to educational level. Caregivers were highly satisfied with training.

There are many fine examples of family day care training programs across the country in local and regional agencies. Family day care training programs consist of other formats, as well. Resource-/toy-lending libraries, for example, are common features.

Family day care training programs consisted of other formats, as well. Resource-/toy-lending libraries were common features, provided by eight programs. Less common were "store-front" neighborhood resource centers for family day care providers (Pine, 1975; Crowe, Pine, & Titus, 1977; Goldsmith, 1979), radio/television broadcasts (Wattenberg, 1977; Goldsmith, 1979; Vartuli, 1989), and formal classes in colleges or vocational-technical schools (Wattenberg, 1977; Goldsmith, 1979; Ungaretti, 1987; Lawrence, Brown, & Bellm, 1989). Thus, as one might expect, the emphasis seems to have been placed on informal training (workshops, discussion groups, or home visits) as opposed to more formal learning experiences. It is significant that so few programs consisted solely of group sessions. Workshops and discussion groups may result in increased knowledge and awareness but are unlikely to result in a change in practices (Kontos, 1988b). To effect change in caregiver practices, then, some other form of training is usually required. Home visiting and resource-lending libraries were the most likely supplements to group sessions. The fact that almost all of the training programs were multifaceted suggests that trainers recognized the need for follow-up and variety in presentation format.

The training program using the most unique format was the Family Day Home Care Provider Program, the independent study program developed by the Texas Agricultural Extension Service (Marshall, 1987), which consisted of a study manual and videotapes. Each of the four chapters of the study manual was complemented by a corresponding 20-minute videotape designed to visually reinforce the concepts presented in the manual. Each chapter in the study manual included a narrative, suggested activities to try, multiple-choice study questions for self-checking, and resource references.

A self-study program can only be successful if the participants actually use the materials. In this program, 75% to 90% of the caregivers completed each chapter of the study manual, and 89% watched all of the videotapes. The majority of caregivers reported spending one to four hours per chapter on the study manual. The study manual was more likely to be rated "very helpful" (94%) than were the videotapes (53%). The reports of the caregivers seemed to confirm that they used the self-study materials, and more than 75% reported that they liked the self-study format and not having to go to meetings.

Training intensity

No form of training is likely to be effective if it is delivered in such small doses that its potential impact is weakened. For instance, weekly as opposed to monthly home visits to family day care providers might be expected to have a more positive effect. Likewise, a single one-hour group session would probably have a different effect than would a series of six weekly sessions, even if the content is similar. Thus, we must examine the format of training in the context of its intensity.

Traditionally, training of any type has involved the trainees going to the trainer in groups. The success of group meetings for family day care training purposes is partially determined by whether caregivers will attend. Two important factors that influence attendance at group meetings are the number and length of meetings. The number of group meetings included in the training programs reviewed here varied from 1 (Kilmer, 1979) to 13 (Jones & Meisels, 1987), with the exception of college courses, which met more often (e.g., Ungaretti, 1987). Most of the programs with group meetings held 4 to 7, varying in length from 90 minutes to three hours. Needless to say, the shorter sessions were more likely to be discussion groups, while the longer sessions tended to be workshops offering a more didactic approach to training. With several exceptions (e.g., Rauch & Crowell, 1974; Kontos, 1988b), the group meetings were held once or twice a month over a several-month period, rather than weekly.

Scheduling, another influential factor in the success of group meetings, was not consistently mentioned in program descriptions. It appears, however, that most of the meetings were scheduled on weekday evenings and a few on Saturday mornings. One program that scheduled meetings on weekday mornings (Kontos, 1988b) did so only because funding for substitutes was available. Another (Goldsmith, 1979) provided child care for the children caregivers brought with them.

When trainers go individually to trainees for home visits, frequency of contact must be determined by balancing the desired amount of change in individual caregiver behavior and the overall need of caregivers in the community for some outside contact. Home visits, with two exceptions (Howes et al., 1988; Kontos, 1988b), occurred once or twice a month. Howes et al. scheduled home visits either every three weeks or every six weeks, depending on the group. Kontos conducted weekly home visits. Although weekly home visits may be desirable for maximum follow-up and continuity, they are time consuming and reduce the number of caregivers that can be trained. Most training programs that included home visits as a component placed a higher priority on reaching a sizable number of caregivers than on follow-up and continuity.

How long the training program continues is another aspect of training intensity. Among these 19 programs, length of training varied from short-term to ongoing. Short-term training programs included the Texas home-study

The most consistent result of training is caregiver satisfaction with it. Group meetings with family day care providers are apparently not an effective strategy for changing their attitudes. The results of some studies suggest that home visiting can be an effective way to improve overall quality of care, even if the visiting relates only to lending toys from a toy-lending library.

A written self-study program can only be successful if the participants read the materials.

program (Marshall, 1987) that lasted four weeks (one per chapter in the study manual) and another home visiting program that encompassed three visits in three weeks (Machida, 1990). Training programs that involved group meetings tended to be stretched across 6 to 12 months, whether or not they also involved home visits or other components. Ongoing training programs were not typical, but included one home-visit program (Rubin, 1974) and one program based in a resource center (Pine, 1975; Crowe, Pine, & Titus, 1977). Overall, it appears that neither short-term nor ongoing training are the norm. Instead, training is typically distributed across one year or less (probably highly dependent on the influx of funds to pay for these activities).

Training content

Although several of the training programs indicated that the content of their program was individually determined, there was a substantial amount of consistency in the content of the programs that did specify content. Not surprisingly, the most frequently covered topics were health/safety/nutrition, child development, guidance or behavior management, working with parents, business practices, and (for three programs) caring for atypical children. Selecting and planning activities for children and infant care were topics included by several programs.

Content did not appear to vary by format because most programs tried to cover the same material in different formats to reinforce the concepts. For instance, the Texas home-study program (Marshall, 1987) included videotapes covering the same topics as each of the study guide chapters. Similarly, Vartuli (1989) included radio broadcasts that covered the same topics as the group sessions and the home visits. Clearly, multifaceted training was used to extend the depth rather than the breadth of information covered.

Effects of training

Describing the format, intensity, and content of training tells us little or nothing about whether or not the training was effective. Training programs have been evaluated on a variety of criteria (e.g., helpfulness, increased knowledge, attitude change, and behavior change), using a variety of methods (e.g., self-report, observation, test, or questionnaire). For instance, some programs that evaluated caregiver behavior changes after training relied on self-report, while others used observation. Attitude change was sometimes measured by simply asking the caregiver if her attitude was different as a result of training. In other cases, attitude change was measured by administering a questionnaire designed to assess caregiver attitudes. This section is organized around the evaluation criteria, with reference made to the method of training and of evaluation. Greater weight will be given to evaluation results obtained by objective, unbiased methods.

Satisfaction with/helpfulness of training

Programs concerned with these aspects of training generally received subjective impressions from family day care providers concerning the training program. Invariably, the majority of caregivers trained were satisfied with the program or indicated that it was helpful (Radin, 1970; Colbert & Enos, 1976; Goldsmith, 1979; Kilmer, 1979; Marshall, 1987; Kontos, 1988b; Vartuli, 1989; Machida, 1990). Caregivers' uniformly positive impressions of their training experiences indicate that satisfaction and helpfulness are not good distinguishing characteristics between training programs of various types and of differing quality. Although the fact that caregivers are satisfied with training and perceive it to be helpful is important, knowing whether caregivers change what they think or do as a result of training is equally important.

Knowledge and attitudes

Many of the training programs used objective tests to evaluate changes in caregivers' knowledge of and attitudes toward child development or child care. For the most part, the tests were administered prior to training and again after the completion of training without evaluating a comparison group of caregivers. Most of the results of these evaluations indicated that family day care providers' knowledge of children and child care increased after training (Rauch & Crowell, 1974; Pine, 1975; Colbert & Enos, 1976; Poresky, 1977; Kaplan & Smock, 1982; Jones & Meisels, 1987; Marshall, 1987; Vartuli,

1989). Several of these evaluations statistically evaluated the increases in test scores to make sure they were not chance results (Poresky, 1977; Jones & Meisels, 1987; Vartuli, 1989) and found that they were not.

Even with statistically significant differences in test scores, however, the improvements in providers' knowledge were modest. For instance, Poresky (1977) found that the group of caregivers trained via workshops by professional trainers significantly increased their knowledge on one part of one test (out of two 2-part tests), but the caregivers trained via workshops by other caregivers did not demonstrate any increase in knowledge. Vartuli (1989) indicated that on a 55-item knowledge and attitude questionnaire, significant differences were present for only 13 of the items. Colbert and Enos (1976) reported that their caregivers increased their test scores from 58% to 74% out of 13 questions possible following a series of 10 workshops. In the Texas home-study training program, caregivers improved their scores on the knowledge test from 55% to 68% after completing the study guide and viewing the videotapes (Marshall, 1987). In a short-term home-visiting program in California, pretests of health care knowledge were not administered. At the end of the training program, however, Machida (1990) found that caregivers' knowledge scores averaged 76%, which is considered barely minimal. Only two programs included a comparison group of untrained caregivers who were administered a test of knowledge (Pine, 1975; Kaplan & Smock, 1982). The results of those evaluations revealed that, in one case, there were no differences between the knowledge of caregivers who were trained (via a resource center, workshops, newsletter, or other method) and those who were not. Moreover, there was no relationship between the level of involvement in training and the caregivers' knowledge. In the other case, the experimental group scored higher on a test of child care information than did the control groups but scored similarly to controls on a test of child care philosophy. As in other studies, increases in test scores were small but statistically significant.

These data suggest that training may have some potential to change caregivers' knowledge of child development and child care. Poor research designs and sketchy reporting of results, however, make it difficult to attribute any knowledge changes to the effects of training. Moreover, when improvements were found, they were typically not substantial. It is impossible to say whether the improvements were small because the training was lacking, because the measure of knowledge did not match the training content, or

The success of group meetings for family day care training purposes is partially determined by whether caregivers will attend them.

simply because short-term training can only be expected to make modest changes in caregivers' knowledge. Research designs that include comparison groups of untrained caregivers and training programs that systematically vary the intensity or method of training are needed in order to understand the change process.

Several training programs focused separately on the childrearing or child care attitudes held by the caregivers (Radin, 1970; Pine, 1975; Colbert & Enos, 1976; Crowe, Pine, & Titus, 1977; Poresky, 1977). All of these programs involved group meetings of some sort, and one (Radin, 1970) also involved home visits. In each case, there was no indication of attitude changes as a result of participation in training. Radin and Pine included a control group of untrained caregivers in their studies and found that their attitudes were no different than those of the trained caregivers. It appears that group meetings with family day care providers are not an effective strategy for changing their attitudes.

Quality of child care

Four studies (Jones & Meisels, 1987; Ungaretti, 1987; Howes, Keeling, & Sale, 1988; Kontos, 1988b) focused on the impact of training on overall child care quality as measured by the Family Day Care Rating Scale (Harms & Clifford, 1989). Although the purpose, nature, and intensity of these four training programs were different, three involved home visiting as a major component of training. In all four studies there were improvements in overall child care quality, although tests of statistical significance were possible in only three (Jones & Meisels, 1987; Ungaretti, 1987; Howes et al., 1988). In the latter three studies, the improvements amounted to .6 to .7 points per item on a seven-point scale. This size of improvement amounts to nearly 20 total points out of a possible 231. In the other study (Kontos, 1988b), total scores improved 50 points on the average, and the average item score increased 1.56 points, from 3.34 (just above *adequate*) to 4.9 (in the *good* category).

Fortunately, two of these studies had control groups. Howes et al. (1988) included a group of caregivers who had been enrolled in a toy loan program but who were not involved in either the more intensive or the less intensive home health training program. Interestingly, in spite of being uninvolved with the training, the control groups' FDCRS scores were significantly higher than pretraining scores of the caregivers in the two training groups. Posttest FDCRS scores for the more intensively trained and the less intensively trained experimental-group caregivers did not differ significantly. These results seemed to suggest that home visiting can be an effective way to improve overall quality of care regardless of the frequency and scope of the visits.

Ungaretti (1987) examined the effectiveness of a college-level course designed for family day care providers to improve overall child care quality. The comparison group of caregivers attended informal group meetings. At the beginning of the study, the two groups were comparable in quality as measured by the FDCRS. At the end of the study, the caregivers attending the college level course had significantly increased their average total score on

There seem to be consistent positive associations between training and behavior. In sponsored and regulated day care homes, one major study indicated that training was associated with more teaching, helping, and dramatic play—and less activity that does not involve interaction with children.

the FDCRS, while the comparison group had not. Thus, the college-level course was judged to be the more effective means for obtaining significant changes in child care quality. Unfortunately, the sample size for this study was extremely small (posttest groups had only eight caregivers each).

The data from three of these studies suggest that home visiting (even when only visits from a toy loan program) has some promise for influencing the overall quality of care provided in family day care homes (even if home visiting is not the preferred method for caregivers [Lawrence et al., 1989]). The other study supports the use of more formal, as opposed to informal, training experiences for family day care providers. Once again, well-designed studies are badly needed that involve control groups receiving no training and comparison groups involved in varying types and intensities of training. Also, a statistically significant improvement in FDCRS scores does not necessarily reflect a "visible" improvement. The large increase in the FDCRS score found in the Kontos (1988b) study was likely to be visible because it amounted to an increase of more than one point per item. To achieve these changes, however, home visits were scheduled weekly—an effort at least twice as intensive as any other program involving home visits. It is conceivable that visible improvements in overall child care quality require very intensive training. If this is true, then training programs designed to improve quality will have to be realistic regarding the numbers of trainees and the cost of training programs.

Caregiver behavior

Surprisingly, perhaps, behavior change typically has not been the primary goal of family day care training programs (if outcomes chosen for evaluation are any indication). The majority of programs addressing behavior change have evaluated this characteristic through caregiver self-report rather than through observations (Pine, 1975; Crowe et al., 1977; Kilmer, 1979; Marshall, 1987; Kontos, 1988b). Needless to say, the objectivity of these self-reports is questionable. The data are much easier to gather, however, and much less threatening to caregivers who may object to being observed by outsiders. Pine (1975) reported that building trust with family day care providers and establishing credibility in the community took precedence over the collection of evaluation data; thus, some trainers have a strong rationale for not

A top priority for a training program has to be overcoming caregivers' initial resistance to training.

---

including observational components in their evaluation. Nonetheless, self-report data cannot take the place of observations when behavior change is a program goal.

With this caveat in mind, we can examine self-reports of caregiver behavior change following training. The training programs that conducted this type of evaluation varied from the Texas home-study program (Marshall, 1987) to workshops and weekly home visits (Kontos, 1988). Four (Pine, 1975; Crowe et al., 1977; Kilmer, 1979; Kontos, 1988b) involved group meetings in some way. In each of the four programs, caregivers reported that they had changed their behavior as a result of training. For instance, in Texas (Marshall, 1987), 72% of the caregivers reported changing *some* practice following the home-study program. Most frequently (72%), the change that was reported was in health and safety practice (e.g., handling emergencies), while a minority of caregivers (35%) reported changing a child development/guidance practice. Just over half (54%) reported change in a business practice. In another training program (Kontos, 1988b), caregivers rated their early intervention skills before and after training from "need to learn" to "a real strength." In pretraining, caregivers rated 68% of their overall skills "need to learn" or "need assistance." After training, only 8.8% of the skills were so rated. The lack of comparison groups for these four studies compounds the initial problem of unobjective self-report data. Thus, we can infer from these studies only that following training, caregivers are likely to report that their behavior has changed.

Only two training programs have included observations of caregiver behavior in their evaluation. Vartuli included an untrained control group in her observations. Colbert and Enos conducted naturalistic observations in family day care trainees' homes during the morning and afternoon both pre- and posttraining. They counted the occurrence of certain target behaviors involving caregivers' interactions with children. There were significant increases after training in the frequency of the following caregiver behaviors: playing with children, positive verbal reinforcement, verbal teaching, verbal social interchange, verbal questioning, and verbal responsiveness. No changes were observed in the frequency of the following caregiver behaviors: physical affection, attending children's needs, attending to personal tasks, constraining and punishing, and negative verbal reinforcement. The behaviors that increased were those the trainers believed they had emphasized during

This can be accomplished through strategies such as using a "buddy system," neighborhood information-sharing parties, outreach by family day care associations and paraprofessionals, and other strategies.

their workshops, while those that did not change were behaviors not addressed at the workshops. Without a comparison or control group, however, changes in caregiver behavior cannot be attributed to the training program.

Because the Vartuli study did include a control group, any observed changes in behavior may be attributed to the training program. A 73-item observation instrument based on family day care CDA competencies was used to compare three groups of caregivers: trained experienced caregivers, trained inexperienced caregivers, and untrained caregivers. Although details of the observation were sketchy, each item was apparently rated by the observer in accordance with the caregiver's behavior. Of the 73 items, the inexperienced caregivers improved on 50, the experienced group improved on 39, and the control group improved on just 22. Unfortunately, however, these differences in the behavior of the three groups of caregivers were not statistically significant; thus, there was no evidence that the training program influenced caregiver behavior.

Not only is there too little observational data, what we have does not confirm the usefulness of training for changing the behavior of family day care providers. In both studies using observation of caregivers to evaluate training, however, changes occurred in the right direction, hinting that training might be an influence on caregiver behavior. More sophisticated research designs and reliable, valid observational systems need to be incorporated into the evaluation of training if we want to determine the efficacy of training for changing family day care providers' behavior.

Retention

The California Child Care Initiative Project (Lawrence et al., 1989) had, as one of its major goals, increasing the retention of newly recruited family day care providers. Training, technical assistance, and support were offered to the new recruits through local resource and referral agencies during their first year, when the turnover rate was presumed to be highest. They were then contacted 12 to 18 months after being recruited in order to determine whether they were still actively providing family day care services. The retention rate was determined by dividing the number of active caregivers by the total number of recruits who were successfully contacted. Based on this method of calculation, the retention rate was an encouraging 69.4%, significantly better than the oft-quoted rate of 41%.

It is important to point out, however, that this retention figure was positively skewed by omitting from the calculation the substantial number of caregivers who could not be reached because their phones were out of service, because there was no answer after three attempts, or because they had failed to seek a license. It was assumed that most of the unreachable caregivers had moved out of the area or had returned to the out-of-home work force. For all practical purposes, then, these caregivers were inactive as far as parents using the local resource and referral agency were concerned (even if, by some chance, they were providing child care in another area of the state or country). If these caregivers had been included in the total number of recruits, the retention rate would have been a more sobering 50%.

Regardless of how the retention rate is calculated, this project has generated valuable information. It is important to remember that the turnover/retention rates calculated in the past for family day care providers did not focus exclusively on turnover/retention in the first year; thus, we have no baseline of comparison for judging first-year retention rates. Even a rate of 50% may be extremely good and only possible with the level of support and assistance provided by the project agencies. A rate of 69% may be nearly miraculous.

Surprisingly, there were no differences between the active and inactive caregivers regarding their involvement in training and support activities. Participation rates were equally high in both groups (nearly 80%). Active caregivers were more likely to have been involved in more than one activity, however. Thus, job commitment among the active caregivers was associated with greater commitment to training.

A key factor distinguishing active from inactive caregivers was income. More than one-third of the inactive caregivers had household incomes of less than $15,000 per year, compared with less than one-fifth of the active caregivers. Nearly one-third of the active caregivers had annual household incomes at or above $35,000. Consistent with these data, inactive caregivers were likely to report that they quit family day care for economic reasons. For this group, even the intensive training, technical assistance, and support offered to them was unable to make family day care economically viable. Lawrence et al. (1989) suggested that financial subsidies for low-income, first-year caregivers may be necessary for optimal retention.

What does training predict?

Although studies of the effects of training have not always had positive or conclusive results, we can gather some solace from the results of family day care studies that have correlated amount or level of training with measures of child care quality as well as with caregiver behaviors. These studies do not evaluate training programs, per se, but instead give us an indication of whether caregivers who have been involved in training are any different from those who have been involved in less training or none at all.

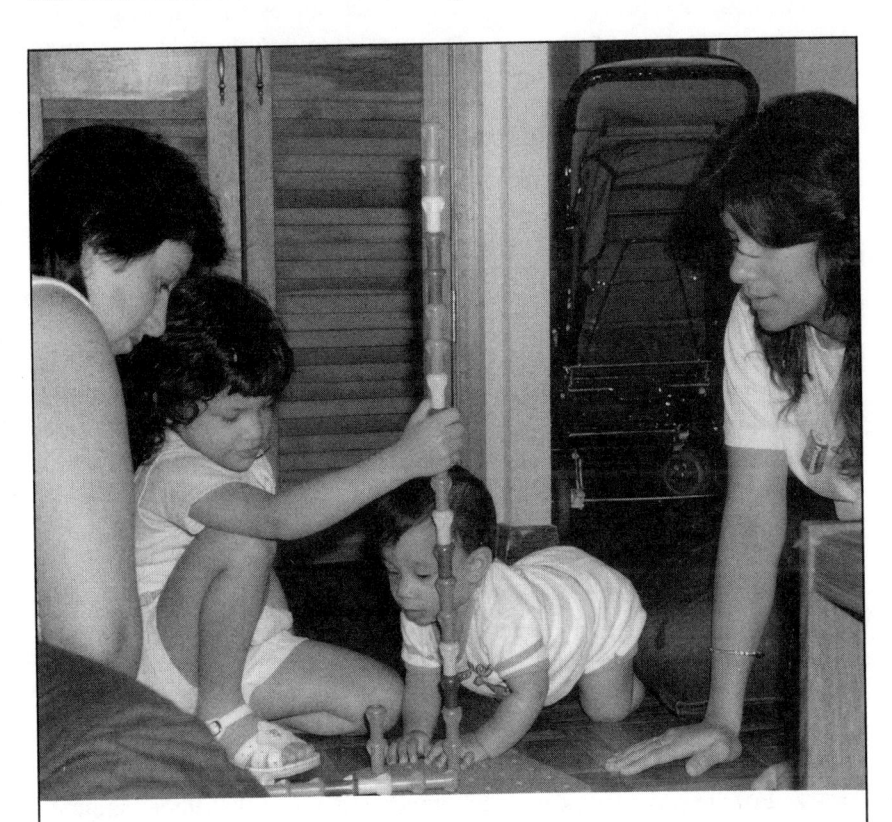

Training is a better predictor of caregiver behavior than is education or experience. Many family day care providers want training; many do not. Workshops and home visits are common forms of family day care training.

> *One researcher recommends that a continuum of training options be developed that require varying amounts of initiative, commitment, and travel.*

The National Day Care Home Study (Divine-Hawkins, 1981; Fosburg, 1982) examined relationships between caregiver training and caregiver behavior, taking into account regulatory status (80% of sponsored caregivers had some training, 30% of regulated caregivers, and 20% of unregulated caregivers). Results revealed that there were consistent positive associations between training and behavior. In sponsored and regulated family day care homes, training was associated with more teaching, helping, and dramatic play—and *less* activity that does not involve interaction with children. Training for sponsored caregivers was also associated with more structured teaching activities. In regulated and unregulated homes, training was associated with more comforting. It may be worthy to note that the sponsored caregivers—the group with the most training—exhibited more associations between training and behavior (eight) than the regulated (five) or unregulated caregivers (four).

Howes (1983) correlated caregiver training with caregiving behaviors among 20 family day care providers. Results revealed that caregivers with more training were more likely to play, highlight or demonstrate a toy, and respond positively to positive toddler bids. (There were no associations between caregiver training and eight other caregiver behaviors.)

In her study of Israeli family day care providers, Rosenthal (1990) documented the contribution of caregivers' amount of pre- and in-service training to the quality of their interaction with children. Caregivers with more training spent less time alone or in preparation and more time with the children in developmentally facilitating interaction.

Lamb, Sternberg, and Knuth (1989) correlated caregiver training in a sample of Swedish family day care providers with their scores on the Belsky and Walker (1980) checklist of positive (e.g., caregiver verbal elaboration) and negative (e.g., caregiver prohibits child action) events. Contrary to expectations, caregiver training was negatively correlated with the Belsky and Walker positive score.

Training has also been found to be positively associated with general measures of family day care quality. Fischer's (1989) study of California family day care providers, discussed previously, found that three variables together explained 70% of the variance in child care quality: training, support, and years of schooling. Training was the best predictor of quality, alone explaining more than 50% of the variance. Similarly, Bollin (1990) reported a significant correlation between family day care provider training and quality of care.

Five of these six correlational studies provide some support for positive associations between caregiver training and caregiver behavior or child care quality. It is important not to infer from correlational data a causal relationship between these variables. If consistently positive associations are found, however, there may be reason to hypothesize that a causal relationship exists between training and caregiver behavior. This hypothesis must then be tested with an experimental design.

Barriers to training: Motivation and recruitment

The issue of motivation for training was first addressed in Chapter 3. Recall that the evidence was somewhat mixed. In other words, for each study indicating that the majority of caregivers are interested in training (Aguirre, 1987; Jones, 1991), there is another study revealing the opposite (Peters, 1972; Eheart & Leavitt, 1986). Any way we interpret the data, there appear to be substantial numbers of caregivers for whom training is a low priority. Thus, the issue of how best to involve family day care providers in training activities is a crucial one. Several studies have addressed this issue.

Based on a multifaceted, two-year training program offered to more than 900 family day care providers in Minnesota, Wattenberg (1977) identified four clusters of family day care providers with different motivations and preferences for training. She found that caregivers in these four clusters varied in the amount and type of training in which they were willing to participate:

• The *traditional* family day care providers, who considered training unimportant and intrusive were most likely to get involved in neighborhood peer groups in which the stated focus was support rather than training.

• The *modernized* family day care provider had a career development orientation and a concern about professionalization with a concomitant interest in all training opportunities. These caregivers were likely to be particularly interested in "accredited coursework" through a college or university and were not deterred by long-term training commitments or participating in training outside the neighborhood.

- *Novice* family day care providers had a "shallow and unstable commitment" to their work and were thus more likely to respond to home-based training.
- A fourth category, the *transitional* family day care provider, was vaguely defined as "emerging into a developmental role for herself." These caregivers responded best initially to short-term commitments and then, as their interest increased, committed themselves to more lengthy training options.

Approximately 50% of the family day care providers were characterized as either traditional or novice. It is important to note that the typology of caregivers was based on the 58% of the family day care providers who involved themselves in some sort of training; 42% of the eligible caregivers chose not to become involved in any type of training.

Of the caregivers who participated in some aspect of training, the majority of those who participated in the most training usually had a driver's license, were more experienced, cared for more children, were experienced caregivers, had previously been employed outside the home, and used the Toy Resource Center. Wattenberg (1977) concluded that the top priority for a training program has to be overcoming caregivers' initial resistance to training. This can be accomplished through strategies such as using a "buddy system," neighborhood information-sharing parties, outreach by family day care associations and paraprofessionals, and other strategies. Results of the training project suggested that resistance is lessened once a caregiver participates in any type of training and that trainers can build on the initial entry into training. Wattenberg (1977) also recommended that a continuum of training options be developed that require varying amounts of initiative, commitment, and travel.

Snow (1982) reported that achieving maximum participation in in-service training depended on accessibility and on the recognition achieved by caregivers for their participation. In a qualitative study of a training and credentialing/accreditation program for family day care providers, Cohen and Modigliani (1990) found that the major obstacles to training were access (cost and location), time and energy, and fear of failure in a "school-like" program. They found that caregivers' motivations for getting involved in the program were intrinsic (e.g,. professionalism, pride, and socializing and networking with peers). None of the respondents in their interviews could identify an extrinsic motivator for caregivers (the exception might be the caregivers who entered training because the regulations in their state required it). Because the caregivers who were in the program were described as among the best and most self-motivated in the community, Cohen and Modigliani questioned whether intrinsic motivation alone is likely to attract other providers for whom the effort involved in becoming credentialed/accredited is a disincentive. One extrinsic motivator they suggested is increased earning power for caregivers who are involved in training and credentialing/accreditation through higher rates, fewer empty spaces, and better business practices (e.g,. late fees, paid vacations, and so forth).

Summary

Workshops and home visits were the most commonly used forms of family day care training. Training programs usually consist of one year or less and involve caregivers once or twice a month. Most frequently covered topics for training are health/safety/nutrition, child development, guidance or behavior management, working with parents, and business practices. The most consistent result of training is caregiver satisfaction with the training. There is very modest evidence of improvements in knowledge/attitudes regarding children or child care and in overall quality of child care. Clear evidence of behavior change can be provided only by caregiver self-reports of changes in caregiving practices. Positive associations have been found between caregiver training and caregiver behavior, and between caregiver training and child care quality. Little is known about other potential outcomes of training (e.g., retention, children's behavior or development, and relations with parents). The typical methodology of these studies makes it nearly impossible to attribute change to training, or to determine relative effectiveness of different forms or intensities of training. There is an overwhelming need for well-designed studies of the effects of training on family day care providers— studies that consider a variety of outcomes. Also, barriers to recruiting caregivers into training must be overcome.

Implications

Does this mean we should stop training family day care providers because we have little or no evidence of its effectiveness? It is true that the studies evaluating training programs show few effects other than caregiver ratings of satisfaction and helpfulness. A prime reason for the paucity of positive effects are inadequacies in the research, however. Thus, we need not say yet that training is ineffective; only that the research has yet to tell us what the potential benefits may be and how best to achieve them. Until we have that type of information, we must rely on the results of a few correlational studies in family day care homes revealing positive relationships between caregiver training and both caregiver behavior and child care quality. We should also rely on the more voluminous research on training among center-based child care staff that shows similar positive influence of training on caregiver behavior and child care quality (e.g., Whitebook, Howes, & Phillips, 1989). Reliance on this research tells us that the more training, the better, and that some training is better than none at all. It cannot tell us the amount of training needed, however, nor can it tell us what and how to train. These questions will only be answered by future research. Programs to train family day care providers must be well-suited to the characteristics of the caregivers to whom they are targeted in order to maximize the likelihood of success.

* * *

NOTE: The section on Barriers to Training was adapted from a chapter on training to appear in "Training and Professionalism in Family Day Care" by S. Kontos & S. Machida with S. Griffin & M. Read. [In D. Peters & A. Pence (Eds.), *Family day care: Current research for informed public policy* (in press). New York: Teachers College Press.]

Chapter 8

Issues and Themes Revisited: Looking to the Future

THIS FINAL CHAPTER WILL BRIEFLY REVIEW what we know about family day care. We will revisit the issues and themes discussed in Chapter 1 in order to assess the status of our knowledge in each area and to suggest likely directions for future programs, policies, and research concerning family day care. In so doing, we can reflect on what questions about family day care have been answered, what questions remain unanswered, and what new questions have arisen as a result of what we know. The answered questions can assist program developers, policymakers, and parents. The new and unanswered questions can direct researchers in their efforts to provide more answers.

What do we know?

One of the frustrations with reviewing large amounts of research on any topic is that in spite of the volume of information available, inconsistencies and omissions still seem to dominate any conclusions that are made. In order to accrue the benefits of research reviews, it is helpful to remind ourselves of what we have learned in spite of the inconsistencies and omissions. The table on page 150 was created with that goal in mind. The content of the table is not all-inclusive but highlights much of what we know about family day care *that is supported by research*. To some extent the information in this table may seem to confirm the obvious because what researchers have documented is also what many practitioners have observed for some time. This is because what we know from research is not necessarily different from what we know from personal experience, common sense, or intuition. The advantage to having our experiences and intuitions confirmed by research is that we can justify generalizing our knowledge to a world larger than our own and using our knowledge to reliably inform policy and practice.

Sometimes research fails to confirm what experience tells us to be true. When this happens it is tempting to "blame the messenger" or to assume that the research has been poorly conducted. When the results of research are counterintuitive, questioning its methodology should without a doubt be the first step in attempting to comprehend their meaning. However, it is equally as important to question whether or not one's personal experiences and intuitions are representative of the "world" of family day care versus a "corner of the world." Results of research that are inconsistent with personal experience do not negate those experiences; they simply remind us of the diversity in which we live and work. It is from this frame of reference that we should interpret the table in this chapter.

Longevity/turnover

Research on longevity, primarily conducted with regulated family day care providers, suggests that the majority have three or more years of experience, while a significant minority have one year or less of experience. Likewise, job commitment among regulated family day care providers appears to be fairly strong. Few caregivers consider their work permanent, but many expect to spend a number of years caregiving. The few studies including unregulated caregivers indicated that they are, on the average, less experienced than are regulated caregivers. We are unlikely to have a completely accurate picture of mechanisms determining longevity and turnover until it is possible to track a large group of regulated and unregulated family day care providers—closely during their first year and then over a period of time. The results of the California Child Care Initiative Project (Lawrence et al., 1989) show clearly how crucial the first year is in determining retention of caregivers, especially for those with lower incomes. Overall, the data are encouraging in that it appears that regulated family day care providers are not "temporary" workers, and a large proportion can be expected to stay with their work for a substantial period of time (years, as opposed to decades).

A positive factor for retention in family day care is that caregivers consistently report liking their work. Even so, it may be unrealistic to expect all family day care providers to make a lifetime commitment to child care (Lawrence et al., 1989). Caregivers whose motivation to do family day care is

---

A positive factor for retention in family day care is that caregivers consistently report liking their work. Even so, it may be unrealistic to expect all family day care providers to make a lifetime commitment to child care. Caregivers whose motivation to do family day care is tied to staying home with or providing companions for their own young children will likely move on to other activities when those motivations no longer remain.

Table. What We Know About Family Day Care and How We Can Make a Difference

Chapter(s)	What We Know	What We Can Do: Caregivers	What We Can Do: Trainers, Advocates, Administrators
1. 2	Some caregivers do not have enough toys and materials.	—Be aware of the benefits of stimulating environments on children. —Take advantage of inexpensive sources of toys and materials.	—Make available toy-/resource-lending libraries. —Include preparation of the environment as a topic for training.
2. 2	Larger group sizes are less advantageous for children than smaller ones.	—Advocate for group-size limitations in family day care regulations. —Self-monitor group size. —Charge fees that make smaller groups feasible financially.	—Assist caregivers in developing fee structures that make small groups financially feasible. —Disseminate information on appropriate adult/child ratios. —Advocate for group-size limitations in family day care regulations.
3. 2	It is more difficult to provide quality care for infants and toddlers.	—Advocate for limitations on the number of infants and toddlers served per adult. —Self-monitor number of infants and toddlers served.	—Advocate for family day care regulations to set limitations on numbers of infants and toddlers per adult served. —Include the special child care needs of infants and toddlers in topics for training.
4. 2	The influence of family day care on children is mediated by family influences.	—Support parents in their childrearing role.	—Advocate for family-friendly social and employment policies. —Include supporting families in topics for training.
5. 2, 7	Training is a better predictor of caregiver behavior than is education or experience.	—Seek training. —Encourage other caregivers to seek training.	—Recruit previously untrained caregivers into training. —Offer accessible training on relevant topics.
6. 3	Most caregivers have substantial experience with children (their own and/or others').	—Learn from the experiences of other caregivers.	—Acknowledge and use this experience to promote new knowledge and awareness. —Recognize and support longevity in family day care.
7. 3	Although caregivers have large informal support networks, only a small proportion of them participate in formal networks such as sponsoring agencies and family day care associations.	—Members of formal support networks must recruit nonmembers.	—Maximize outreach to caregivers, especially those who are unregulated.
8. 3, 7	Some caregivers are reluctant to seek training.	—Willing caregivers must encourage the reluctant ones to seek training.	—Maximize the accessibility of training in terms of cost, location, timing, and content.

#	Statement		
9. 4	Caregivers work long hours for low pay.	—Seek support from other caregivers. —Take paid holidays and vacations. —Advocate for better pay and working conditions for family day care providers.	—Advocate for better pay and working conditions for family day care providers. —Support caregivers and help them support each other. —Include "survival strategies" in topics for training.
10. 4	Regulated caregivers provide higher quality care *on the average*.	—Become regulated. —Encourage unregulated caregivers to become regulated. —Inform unregulated caregivers of the importance of regulation and the ease of compliance.	—Increase accessibility of regulation for caregivers. —Increase public awareness regarding the value of regulation.
11. 4	There is a lack of consensus regarding what *professionalism* means for family day care.	—Exchange opinions with other caregivers and child care professionals. —Get involved with professional organizations.	—Exchange opinions with caregivers and other child care professionals.
12. 4	Many caregivers view teaching and mothering as separate functions.	—Learn how mothering and teaching complement one another.	—Promote a respect and understanding of the compatibility of mothering and teaching.
13. 5	Parents do not necessarily visit family day care homes before enrolling their child.	—Encourage prospective parents to "shop around." —Require a pre-enrollment visit to your family day care home.	—Make resource and referral services accessible to parents. —Provide consumer education for parents.
14. 5	Many caregivers are frustrated in their relations with parents.	—Cultivate an appreciation for diversity. —Cultivate assertiveness skills. —Be supportive of working parents. —Expect working parents to treat *you* as a working parent.	—Include assertiveness training and effective communication in topics for training. —Include relations with parents in topics for training.
15. 6	There is widespread dissatisfaction with present regulatory approaches for family day care.	—Investigate fresh approaches to regulation. —Communicate new ideas with family day care advocates and policymakers.	—Investigate fresh approaches to family day care regulation. —Communicate new ideas with caregivers, other advocates, and policymakers.
16. 7	When family day care providers get involved in training, they like it.	—Seek training.	—Ask previously trained caregivers to help recruit untrained caregivers into training. —Do not assume that training is effective because caregivers like it; other evidence of training success besides caregiver satisfaction is needed.
17. 7	Workshops and home visits are the most common forms of training for family day care providers.	—Be available to attend workshops. —Be open to home visits. —Make trainers aware of more effective, accessible modes of training.	—Choose training formats based on maximizing accessibility and effectiveness rather than what is most common.

tied to staying home with or providing companions for their own young children will likely move on to other activities when those motivations no longer remain. Caregivers whose life experiences and economic needs are well matched with the family day care lifestyle may be more likely to see it as their profession than as a temporary arrangement (Kontos & Riessen, under review). Members of either group have the potential to provide quality care.

Lawrence et al. (1989) astutely pointed out that not all turnover is bad. Some caregivers who perceive themselves as custodial "babysitters" or as just doing a favor for a friend or relative may not be well suited for work in family day care. Little will be gained by encouraging caregivers in this category to continue if they are unlikely to be committed to their work or to provide quality child care. Lawrence et al. suggested that career assessments prior to training and support activities may convince some new caregivers with unrealistic expectations to drop out. This may work for regulated caregivers in communities with resource and referral agencies or family day care associations. For unregulated caregivers and in communities without agencies or associations, entry into family day care is "trial by fire."

The decision to leave family day care appears to frequently be an economic one for both regulated and unregulated caregivers. Thus, technical assistance for caregivers on the business aspects of family day care may be crucial for longevity. To the extent that family day care providers' fees and income are linked to women's earnings in the community, economic issues will continue to be a problem. Unless salary equity at a societal level is addressed, family day care providers will continue to have income problems, regardless of any technical assistance they receive. In other words, maximizing longevity and minimizing turnover among family day care providers will require action within the profession but also by society at large.

Child care as family support

It is not at all clear that family day care is superior to other forms of child care in its ability to support families. Research suggests that scheduling is more flexible when dealing with parents than with centers, but that family day care is not necessarily any closer to home; thus, the convenience factor for family day care is less than imagined. Family day care has been shown to be a more informal setting than center-based care, and, practically speaking, there usually is only one caregiver for parents to get to know. These two factors may set some parents' minds at ease. Of greater concern are the caregivers' reports of frustration in their dealings with parents combined with evidence that communication between caregivers and parents is less than optimal. Nelson (1989) perceptively observed that mothers and caregivers lack mutual understanding. Their interests as users and providers of a service are somewhat incompatible, resulting in a less-than-ideal relationship. Under these circumstances, it should not be surprising that caregivers are frustrated, but it also is unlikely that family day care can function well as a family support mechanism.

The intricacies of parent-caregiver relationships in the context of family day care need to be more fully explored. Perhaps the home setting, for all its warmth and informality, complicates relations between parents and caregivers because it is not "neutral territory" in the same way a center is. It may be easier for parents to arrive or pay late (two key irritants for caregivers) if they see the caregiver as someone who is home anyway, earning "pin money," and not as a professional with a job. By the same token, caregivers may be more sensitive to parents' infringements when they occur in their home than they would be if the infringements occurred elsewhere. Moreover, caregivers must perform a balancing act between two roles that may seem incompatible: mother and businessperson. Overall, the research shows that relationships between parents and caregivers in family day care are complex, but research does not clearly explain why or what needs to be done. Caregivers may benefit from training on relations with parents. More research is needed on the nature of parent-caregiver relations in family day care and the correlates of good versus poor relations. It would also be interesting to know if relations with parents affect a caregivers' longevity.

Regulation

The controversy over appropriate regulatory approaches for family day care is far from over. The prime issue seems to be licensing versus registration. Another key issue is exemption from regulation—whether there should be such a thing and, if so, under what circumstances. The topic of regulation is the least researched area addressed in this book. Consequently, we must rely on governmental statistics and expert opinion, which can be quite useful and informative. They cannot, however, supplant research that systematically addresses the impact of varying regulatory approaches on the quality and availability of family day care. Research of this type is difficult and expensive. Because we cannot expect states to allow experimentation with regulations (not only is it intrusive, but most states appear to be satisfied with their present approach), "natural experiments" must be relied upon to supply needed data. This might involve comparing the supply of regulated family day care (amount, quality based on regulatable criteria, and so forth) in two demographically similar states with different regulatory approaches. Problems with such approaches include the likelihood that extraneous factors differentiating the target states will influence the results, and the constant issue of determining the impact of regulation on the generally inaccessible population of unregulated caregivers. Confounding factors can sometimes be statistically controlled, and expensive, time-consuming data collection methods (e.g., random digit dialing) can be called upon to reduce the accessibility problem. The fact remains that empirical research on regulation is likely to remain scarce because of its difficulty and expense.

Training and professionalism

Much has been written describing the training background of family day care providers and programs designed to do the training. It is clear that family day care providers are unlikely to be formally trained, and their opportunities for or desire to participate in informal training are frequently minimal. It is not clear that training changes caregivers' practices; good experimental data are lacking, and we are reliant on correlational studies that typically find positive associations between amount of training and frequency of appropriate behavior. As we learned in Chapter 5, more rigorously designed research on training is badly needed.

A more basic issue needs to be resolved first, however, before we can appropriately interpret research on training and what it means for professionalism in family day care. It is not just family day care providers who suffer from a "muddled" self-image of mother versus child care professional, nurturer versus wage earner; the child care profession in general has yet to speak with one voice regarding where family day care is located on the home-center continuum.

To some it may seem obvious. A family day care home is just that—a home—and should not emulate a center or a school (e.g., Sale, 1973a, b). The strength of family day care lies in its difference from "school-like" approaches —in its flexibility, intimacy, familiarity, and congruence with family values. Caregivers need support and improved status, not teaching skills.

Others (e.g., Howes & Sakai, in press) believe that the reality of daily life as a family day care provider bears little resemblance to family life in the 1990s. Long hours with large groups of children (compared to the size of a typical family) and the concomitant additional household duties make it difficult to imagine that children are getting optimal amounts of attention. Indeed, research shows that group size has a negative impact on caregiver behavior (see Chapter 5). Infants and toddlers may even experience better caregiver/child ratios in centers than in family day care homes in many states. From this perspective, it seems doubtful that the skills of mothering (as wonderful as they might be) are sufficient for a developmentally appropriate family day care environment. More "teacher-like" skills are seen as desirable.

Depending on one's perspective on family day care, the purpose of training—and thus the criteria for its success—will vary. Research investigating different forms of family day care (varying in structure, group size, age mix, and so forth) and their relative impact on children and families could help us to determine what family day care's "best suit" is and, in turn, the appropriate focus for the content and outcome of training.

Quality

Quality in family day care varies, as one might expect, but research has shown that, on the average, the quality is adequate (in regulated homes). Similar results were found for quality in child care centers in the National Child Care Staffing Study (NCCSS [Whitebook, Howes, & Phillips, 1989]). Adequate quality can be viewed from a "half full" versus "half empty" perspective. The NCCSS took the "half empty" perspective in its expressions of concern over center-based child care that was typically "barely adequate" in quality. It is hard to find child care professionals advocating for merely adequate quality (although there has been some discussion of distinctions between "good" and "good enough" quality care). The NCCSS stance reflects the belief that our children deserve good or excellent care. Because the desire for quality child care for all children is not restricted to center-based settings, it would not be unreasonable for child care professionals to express some concern at the typical level of quality in regulated family day care homes. Such concern is heightened, presumably, for unregulated family day care because the limited data base indicates that unregulated family day care is typically lower in quality than is regulated family day care.

The "half full" perspective may be taken by those who, given the background and working conditions of typical regulated family day care providers, are amazed that adequate-quality care is typical when poor-quality might as easily be. It is reasonable to argue that we are lucky to have even adequate quality when, unlike caregivers in countries such as France and Denmark (Richardson & Marx, 1989; Corsini, 1991), caregivers in many areas of this country operate largely outside of professional supervision and support, factors that have been shown to make a significant difference in quality in family day care (Rosenthal, 1990). Thus, it is easy to be of two minds about typical quality in regulated family day care. Based on available research, concern is probably warranted regarding quality in unregulated family day care.

An area that has yet to be investigated is whether caregivers accredited by NAFDC or with a CDA credential are providing higher quality care than their peers who are neither so accredited nor credentialed. Preliminary impressions indicate that they do provide higher quality care (Cohen & Modigliani, 1990), but no comparative observations have been conducted. We also need a better sense of the characteristics of caregivers who are likely to seek accreditation or credentialing. Relatively few have yet sought accreditation or credentialing, and they are geographically dispersed. Consequently, a study of this type would be complicated and expensive.

Available research fails to provide a picture of the impact of family day care quality on children's development that is sufficiently clear to be directly translated into policy or practice because the studies have been conducted with children of different ages in areas that have different regulatory climates. Another study of the scope of the NDCHS is needed that focuses on the impact of quality. The bottom line for policy ought to be defining the floor of family day care quality below which children are harmed. It would also be useful to understand the relative impact (if any) on children of adequate versus good or excellent care. Needless to say, none of these quality issues can be illuminated without also examining how family factors act as mediators between the effects of quality and child outcomes.

Compensation and affordability

Family day care has been traditionally regarded as more affordable than center-based care. Recent research indicates that this may not be an accurate assumption. Although it is true that centers invariably charge fees while some caregivers provide free family day care for relatives or friends (Waite et al., 1991), when parents do pay, their fees are typically comparable with those of center-based programs (Kisker et al., 1989). Thus, the issue of affordability is similar for family day care and for center-based care.

At the heart of the issue, of course, is the balance between adequate compensation for caregivers and affordability for parents. Because family day care providers are their own bosses, theoretically they are free to charge whatever they must to earn a fair wage. Research has documented, however, that family day care providers consciously set fees according to parents' ability to pay (Zinsser, 1990; Nelson, 1991a), not based on what is a fair wage for their work. Group size, not fees, is more likely to be altered according to the fair wage criterion. Thus, compensation and affordability are linked to quality because group size is a key quality indicator. The link between compensation and group size makes group size limitations in state child care regulations a bitter pill to swallow for some regulated caregivers who need to earn more money and believe they are capable of caring for more children than the state will allow. Compensation is also linked to turnover or retention because caregivers are likely to name economics as a major factor in dropping out of family day care in the first year (Lawrence et al., 1989). Resolving the compensation issue would obviously assist in the resolution of several other crucial child care problems. Unfortunately, available data describe the problem better than they suggest solutions.

Descriptions of the compensation/affordability conundrum and its link with quality and regulation are useful to the extent that they can inform parents and policymakers, many of whom are not yet aware of the problem. Informing parents and policymakers is an important first step in obtaining positive change. Meanwhile, the child care community needs to formulate proposals for changes in present family day care funding systems in order to promote both fair wages and quality care while, if deemed desirable, maintaining the entrepreneurial nature of family day care. This is a tall order, to be sure, but emerging from the present vicious cycle will require no less.

Looking to the future

As child care issues in general have come to the forefront nationally, so has family day care emerged from the shadows of child care into the limelight. For child care professionals, this is a time when initiatives designed to enhance family day care for caregivers and families abound. These initiatives (e.g., Lawrence et al., 1989; Cohen & Modigliani, 1990) are increasing our insights into common predictors of success for family day care providers in terms of longevity and quality of services. Training, support, and technical assistance are all ingredients in the recipe for success being developed by these initiatives. Those initiatives that have the foresight to keep detailed records of their activities and the participants in order to measure their own effectiveness will contribute immeasurably to our knowledge about family day care.

Scholars initially discovered family day care in the early 1970s. It appears that as time passes, the energy and creativity going into family day care research more closely matches that for center-based care. Research designs have become more sophisticated as the research questions have become more complex and better conceptualized. Rarely do we now see simple comparisons of family day care with center-based care, as if the differences or similarities are important or meaningful in and of themselves. Family characteristics and regulatory climate, for instance, are more consistently taken into account when designing studies and interpreting their results. In spite of the progress made in the area of family day care research, there is much to be done to answer policy-relevant questions, and we face great challenges as we work to obtain these answers.

One challenge is increasing collaborative activities between family day care scholars and practitioners. The questions that need answers require the expertise and insights of both groups and from multiple disciplines, not just early childhood education. Our success in meeting the challenge of collaboration will depend on the ability of scholars and practitioners to value one another's work but also to value and take advantage of their interdependence.

Another challenge is helping family day care providers to feel comfortable with trainers and researchers in their homes. Without the trust and cooperation of the caregivers themselves, it is impossible to deliver training, support, or technical assistance to them, much less evaluate the effects of such efforts. Any trainer or researcher of family day care, no matter how friendly and well-meaning, however, can tell stories of their difficulties gaining entry to family day care homes. Changing this state of affairs will require patience, sensitivity, and most likely the assistance of other caregivers who have overcome their reluctance to being involved with the larger world of family day care.

Perhaps the greatest challenge will be seeing that program development and research on family day care is properly funded. It is encouraging to see public-private partnerships such as the California Child Care Initiative Project funding family day care programs on a large-scale basis. Adequate funding in the future will require access to local, state, and federal governmental dollars, as well as assistance from philanthropic and advocacy organizations. More than that is needed, however. Discussing parent education and support programs, Powell (1989) suggested that in addition to funds for these service activities, networks that link practitioners and scholars are necessary. Such networks are also needed for family day care scholars and practitioners. To maximize the impact of funding for services, it is crucial that practitioners and scholars communicate with one another regarding family day care program developments and research.

References

Abbott-Shim, M. S., & Kaufman, M. (1986). *Characteristics of family day care providers.* Atlanta, GA: Georgia State University. (ERIC Document Reproduction Service No. ED 287 585)

Adams, D. (1984). Family day care registration: Is it deregulation or more feasible state public policy? *Young Children, 39*(4), 74–77.

Adams, D. (1989, April). *Understanding the image of family day care.* Paper presented at the Save the Children National Family Day Care Technical Assistance Conference, Atlanta, GA.

Adams, G. C. (1990). *Who knows how safe?: The status of state efforts to ensure quality child care.* Washington, DC: Children's Defense Fund.

Aguirre, B. E. (1987). Educational activities and needs of family day care providers in Texas. *Child Welfare, 66,* 459–465.

Anderson, E. A. (1986). Family day care provision: A legislative response. *Child Care Quarterly, 15,* 6–14.

Atkinson, A. M. (1987). Fathers' participation and evaluation of family day care. *Family Relations, 36,* 146–151.

Atkinson, A. M. (1988). Providers' evaluations of the effect of family day care on family relationships. *Family Relations, 37,* 399–404.

Belsky, J., & Walker, A. (1980). *Infant-toddler center spot observation system.* Unpublished manuscript, Pennsylvania State University, Department of Human Development and Family Studies, University Park, PA.

Bollin, G. G. (under review). *An investigation of turnover among family day care providers.*

Bollin, G. G. (1989, March). *Diversity in attitudes about family day care among sponsored family day care providers.* Paper presented at the annual meeting of the American Educational Research Association, San Francisco, CA.

Bollin, G. G. (1990). *An investigation of turnover among family day care providers.* Paper presented at the annual meeting of the American Educational Research Association, Boston, MA.

Bollin, G. G., & Whitehead, L. C. (1991, April). *The enigma of family day care provider job satisfaction.* Paper presented at the American Educational Research Association Annual Conference, Chicago, IL.

Brout, B. L., & Krabbenhoft, K. (1977). The Red Hook Family Day Care training program. *Young Children, 32*(5), 49–52.

Bryant, B., Harris, M., & Newton, D. (1980). *Children and minders.* Ypsilanti, MI: High/Scope Press.

Bureau of the Census. (1990). *Who's minding the kids? Child care arrangements 1986–87.* (Current Population Reports, Series P–70, No. 20). Washington, DC: U. S. Government Printing Office.

California Child Care Resource and Referral Network. (1988). *The California child care initiative project.* San Francisco, CA: Author.

Children's Foundation. (1989). *Issues in the regulation of family day care.* Washington, DC: Author.

Children's Foundation. (1990). *Family day care licensing study.* Washington, DC: Author.

Clarke-Stewart, A. (1984). Day care: A new context for research and development. In M. Perlmutter (Ed.), *Minnesota symposium on child psychology* (pp. 61–100). Minneapolis: University of Minnesota Press.

Clarke-Stewart, K. A. (1986). Family day care: A home away from home? *Children's Environments Quarterly, 3,* 34–46.
Clarke-Stewart, K. A. (1987). Predicting child development from child care forms and features: The Chicago study. In D. Phillips (Ed.), *Quality in child care: What does research tell us?* (pp. 21–41). Washington, DC: National Asociation for the Education of Young Children.
Clarke-Stewart, K. A., & Gruber, C. P. (1984). Day care forms and features. In R. Ainslie (Ed.), *The child and the day care setting: Qualitative variations and development* (pp. 35–62). New York: Praeger.
Class, N. E. (1980). Some reflections on the development of child day care faculty licensing. In S. Kilmer (Ed.), *Advances in Early Education and Day Care* (Vol. 1, pp. 3–18). Greenwich, CT: JAI Press.
Cochran, M. M. (1977). A comparison of group day and family child-rearing patterns in Sweden. *Child Development, 48,* 702–707.
Cochran, M. M., & Gunnarsson, L. (1985). A follow-up study of group day care and family-based childrearing patterns. *Journal of Marriage and the Family, 47,* 297–309.
Cohen, N. (1990). *Highlights of the National Family Day Care Project.* New York: National Council of Jewish Women.
Cohen, N., & Modigliani, K. (1990). *The family to family evaluation report.* New York: Families and Work Institute.
Colbert, J. C., & Enos, M. M. (1976). *Educational services for home day caregivers: Final report.* (Report No. RU–TR–12) Chicago, IL: Roosevelt University, College of Education. (ERIC Document Reproduction Service No. ED 134 341)
Corsini, D. (1991). Family day care in Denmark: A model for the United States? *Young Children, 46*(5), 10–15.
Council for Early Childhood Professional Recognition. (1989). *Family day care providers: Child Development Association assessment system and competency standards.* Washington, DC: CDA National Credentialing Program.
Cox, D., & Richarz, S. (1987). *Traditional and modernized characteristics of registered and unregistered family day care providers.* Pullman, WA: Washington State University. (ERIC Document Reproduction Service No. ED 290 577)
Crowe, N. D., Pine, B. A., & Titus, J. (1977, July–August). An educational progam for family day care mothers: A pilot project. *Children Today,* 6–10.
Culkin, M., Morris, J., & Hughes, S. (1991). Quality and the true cost of child care. *Journal of Social Issues, 37,* 71–86.
Deiner, P. L., & Whitehead, L. C. (1988). Levels of respite care as a family support system. *Topics in Early Childhood Special Education, 8*(2), 51–61.
Divine-Hawkins, P. (1981). *Family day care in the United States: Executive summary.* (Final Report of the National Day Care Home Study) (Report No. DHHS–OHDS–80–30287). Washington, DC: Administration of Children, Youth and Families. (ERIC Document Reproduction Service No. ED 211 224)
Dunn, L., & Kontos, S. (1989, April). *Influence of family day care quality and childrearing attitudes on children's play in family day care.* Paper presented at the biennial meeting of the Society for Research in Child Development, Kansas City, MO.
Eheart, B. K., & Leavitt, R. L. (1986). Training day care home providers: Implications for policy and research. *Early Childhood Research Quarterly, 1,* 119–132.
Eheart, B. K., & Leavitt, R. L. (1989). Family day care: Discrepancies between intended and observed caregiving practices. *Early Childhood Research Quarterly, 4,* 145–162.
Emlen, A.C. (1973). Slogans, slots, and slander: The myth of day care need. *American Journal of Orthopsychiatry, 43,* 23–36.

Emlen, A. C., Donoghue, B. A., & Clarkson, Q. D. (1974). *The stability of the family day care arrangement: A longitudinal study*. Portland, OR: Regional Research Institute for Human Services.

Emlen, A. C., Donoghue, B. A., & LaForge, R. (1971). *Child care by kith: A study of the family day care relationships of working mothers and neighborhood caregivers* (2nd ed.). Portland, OR: Regional Research Institute for Human Services.

Enarson, E. (1991). Experts and caregivers: Perspectives on underground day care. In E. Abel & M. Nelson (Eds.), *Circles of care: Work and identity in women's lives* (pp. 233–245). Albany, NY: State University of New York Press.

Fiene, R., & Melnick, S. A. (1991, April). *Quality assessment in early childhood programs: A multi-dimensional approach*. Paper presented at the annual meeting of the American Educational Research Association, Chicago, IL.

Fischer, J. L. (1989). *Family day care: Factors influencing the quality of caregiving practices*. Unpublished doctoral dissertation, University of Illinois, Urbana, IL.

Floge, L. (1985). The dynamics of child-care use and some implications for women's employment. *Journal of Marriage and the Family, 47*, 143–154.

Fosburg, S. (1982). Family day care: The role of the surrogate mother. In L. Laosa & I. Sigel (Eds.), *Families as learning environments for children* (pp.223–260). New York: Plenum.

Fuqua, R. W., & Labensohn, D. (1986). Parents as consumers of child care. *Family Relations, 35*, 295–303.

Fuqua, R. W., & Schieck, R. (1989). Child care resource and referral programs and parents' search for quality child care. *Early Childhood Research Quarterly, 4*, 357–365.

Glantz, F. B. (1989, November). *The market for family day care: Myths and reality*. Paper presented at the annual meeting of the Association for Public Policy and Management, Washington, DC.

Goelman, H. (1986). The language environments of family day care. In S. Kilmer (Ed.), *Advances in Early Education and Day Care*, (Vol. 4, pp.153–179). Greenwich, CT: JAI Press.

Goelman, H., Shapiro, E., & Pence, A. R. (1990). Family environment and family day care. *Family Relations, 39*, 14–19.

Golden, M., Rosenbluth, M., Grossi, H., Policare, H., Freeman, H., & Brownlee, E. (1979). *The New York City infant day care study: A comparative study of licensed group and family infant day care programs and the effects of these programs on children and their families*. New York, NY: Medical and Health Research Association of New York City, Inc. (ERIC Document Reproduction Service No. ED 167 260)

Goldsmith, M. J. (1979, July–August). The Rhode Island connection: A family day care training program. *Children Today*, 2–5.

Gramley, M. (1990, April). *Providers' role perceptions and the design and delivery of family day care services*. Paper presented at the annual meeting of the American Educational Research Association, Boston, MA.

Greenspan, S. I., Silver, B., & Allen, M. G. (1977). A psychodynamically oriented group training program for early childhood care givers. *American Journal of Psychiatry, 134*, 1104–1108.

Harms, T., & Clifford, R. (1989). *Family day care rating scale*. New York: Teachers College Press.

Harrold, J. D. (1976). *Day care licensing improvement project* (Final report). Lansing, MI: Michigan State University, Department of Social Services. (ERIC Document Reproduction Service No. ED 129 438)

Hayes, C. D., Palmer, J. L., & Zaslow, M. J. (Eds.). (1990). *Who cares for America's children?* Washington, DC: National Academy Press.

Hofferth, S. L. (1989). What is the demand for and supply of child care in the United States? *Young Children, 44*(5), 28–33.

Hofferth, S. L., & Brayfield, A. (1991, April). *Child care in the United States: 1990*. Paper presented at the biennial meeting of the Society for Research in Child Development, Seattle, WA.

Hofferth, S. L., & Phillips, D. A. (1987, August). Child care in the United States, 1970 to 1995. *Journal of Marriage and the Family, 49,* 559–571.

Hofferth, S. L. & Phillips, D. A. (1991). Child care policy research. *Journal of Social Issues, 47,* 1–13.

Hofferth, S. L., & Wissoker, D. A. (1990, February). *Quality, price, and income on child care choice*. Paper presented at the annual meeting of the Population Association of America, Toronto, Canada.

Howes, C. (1983). Caregiver behavior in center and family day care. *Journal of Applied Developmental Psychology, 4,* 99–107.

Howes, C. (1987). Social competency with peers: Contributions from child care. *Early Childhood Research Quarterly, 2,* 155–167.

Howes, C., Keeling, K., & Sale, J. (1988). *The home visitor: Improving quality in family day care homes*. Unpublished manuscript.

Howes, C., & Rubenstein, J. L. (1981). Toddler peer behavior in two types of day care. *Infant Behavior and Development, 4,* 387–393.

Howes, C., & Rubenstein, J. L. (1985). Determinants of toddlers' experience in day care: Age of entry and quality of setting. *Child Care Quarterly, 14,* 140–151.

Howes, C., & Sakai, L. M. (in press). Family day care for infants and toddlers. In D. Peters & A. Pence (Eds.), *Family day care: Current research for informed public policy*. New York: Teachers College Press.

Howes, C., & Stewart, P. (1987). Child's play with adults, toys, and peers: An examination of family and child-care influences. *Developmental Psychology, 23*(3), 423–430.

Hughes, R. (1985). The informal help-giving of home and center childcare providers. *Family Relations, 34,* 359–366.

Innes, R., Woodman, J., Banspach, S., Thompson, L., & Inwald, C. (1982). A comparison of the environments of day care centers and group day care homes for three-year-olds. *Journal of Applied Developmental Psychology, 3,* 41–56.

Johnson, L. C. (1981). Planning the day care home environment for young children. *Environmental Design Research Association, 12,* 294–300.

Jones, K. F. (1991). *Job satisfaction, commitment to professionalism, and perceived support systems in family day care providers*. Unpublished master's thesis, National-Louis University, Evanston, IL.

Jones, S. N., & Meisels, S. J. (1987). Training family day care providers to work with special needs children. *Topics in Early Childhood Special Education, 7*(1), 1–12.

Kahn, M., & Kamerman, S. (1987). *Child care: Facing the hard choices*. Dover, MA: Auburn House.

Kamerman, S., & Kahn, A. (1981). *Child care, family benefits, and working parents*. New York: Columbia University Press.

Kaplan, M. G., & Smock, S. M. (1982, September). *An effective training approach for child day care providers*. Paper presented at the annual meeting of the American Psychological Association, Washington, DC. (ERIC Document Reproduction Service No. ED 223 337)

Kilmer, S. (1979). Family day care training: A home-based model. *Young Children, 34*(3), 12–19.

Kisker, E. E., Maynard, R., Gordon, A., & Strain M. (1989). *The child care challenge: What parents need and what is available in three metropolitan areas*. Princeton, NJ: Mathematica Policy Research, Inc.

Kivikink, R., & Schell, B. (1987). Demographic, satisfaction, and commitment profiles of day care users, nursery school users, and babysitter users in a medium-sized Canadian city. *Child & Youth Care Quarterly, 16*, 116–130.

Klein, R. P. (1985). Caregiving arrangements by employed women with children under 1 year of age. *Developmental Psychology, 21*(3), 403–406.

Kontos, S. (1988a, April). *Job satisfaction and career development in family day care.* Paper presented at the annual meeting of the American Educational Research Association, New Orleans, LA.

Kontos, S. (1988b). Family day care as an integrated early intervention setting. *Topics in Early Childhood Special Education, 8*, 1–14.

Kontos, S. (1989). *Predictors of job satisfaction and child care quality in family day care.* Paper presented at the annual meeting of the American Educational Research Association, San Francisco, CA.

Kontos, S. (1990). *Children, families, and child care: The search for connections.* Paper presented at the annual meeting of the American Educational Research Association, Boston, MA.

Kontos, S., & Riessen, J. (under review). Predictors of job satisfaction, job stress, and job commitment in family day care providers.

Kontos, S., & Well, W. (1986). Attitudes of caregivers and the day care experiences of families. *Early Childhood Research Quarterly, 1*, 47–67.

Lamb, M. E., Sternberg, K. J., & Knuth, N. (1989, April). *Quality of family day care and the development of peer social skills.* Paper presented at the biennial meeting of the Society for Research in Child Development, Kansas City, MO.

Lamb, M. E., Hwang, C. P., Bookstein, F. L., Broberg, A., Hult, G., & Frodi, M. (1988). Determinants of social competence in Swedish preschoolers. *Developmental Psychology, 24*, 58–70.

Lamb, M. E., Hwang, C. P., Broberg, A., & Bookstein, F. L. (1988). The effects of out-of-home care on the development of social competence in Sweden: A longitudinal study. *Early Childhood Research Quarterly, 3*, 379–402.

Lawrence, M., Brown, J., & Bellm, D. (1989). *Helping family day care providers stay in the business: Retention strategies from the California Child Care Initiative.* San Francisco, CA: California Child Care Resource and Referral Network.

Leavitt, R. L. (1987). *Invisible boundaries: An interpretive study of parent-provider relationships.* Champaign-Urbana, IL: University of Illinois. (ERIC Document Reproduction Service No. ED 299 035)

Leavitt, R. L. (1991). Family day care licensing: Issues and recommendations. *Child and Youth Care Forum, 20*, 243–254.

Long, F., & Garduque, L. (1987). Continuity between home and family day care: Caregivers' and mothers' perceptions and children's social experience. In D. L. Peters & S. Kontos (Eds.), *Continuity and discontinuity of experience in child care* (Vol. 2, pp. 69–90). *Annual Advances in Applied Developmental Psychology.* Norwood, NJ: Ablex.

Long, F., Peters, D. L., & Garduque, L. (1985). Continuity between home and day care: A model for defining relevant dimensions of child care. In I. Sigel (Ed.), *Annual advances in applied developmental psychology* (Vol. 1, pp. 131–170). Norwood, NJ: Ablex.

Machida, S. (1990). In-home health education for family day care providers: A rural community-based project. *Child & Youth Care Quarterly, 19*, 271–288.

Majeed, A. (1983). *Casper family day care study.* Casper, WY: Nutrition and Child Development, Inc. (ERIC Document Reproduction Service No. ED 243 570)

Mansfield, A. M. (1986). *Professionalism in family day care.* Unpublished master's thesis, Pacific Oaks College, Pasadena, CA. (ERIC Document Reproduction Service No. ED 315 180)

Marshall, M. G. (1987). *A family day home care provider program.* College Station, TX: Texas Agricultural Extension Service.

Mason, K., & Kuhlthau, K. (1989). Determinants of child care ideals among mothers of preschool-aged children. *Journal of Marriage and the Family, 51,* 593–603.

Melnick, S. A., & Fiene, R. (1990, April). *Licensure and program quality in early childhood and child care programs.* Paper presented at the annual meeting of the American Educational Research Association, Boston, MA.

Modigliani, K. (no date). *Assessing the quality of family child care: A comparison of five instruments.* Hayward, CA: Mervyn's Public Affairs Office.

Morgan, G. (1980). Can quality family day care be achieved through regulation? In S. Kilmer (Ed.), *Advances in early education and day care,* (Vol. 1, pp. 91–102). Greenwich, CT: JAI Press.

Morgan, G. (1985). The government perspective on quality. In L. Schweinhart & D. Weikart (Eds.), *Quality in early childhood programs: Four perspectives* (pp. 10–30). Ypsilanti, MI: High/Scope Educational Research Foundation.

Moss, P. (1987). *A review of childminding research.* London: University of London Institute of Education.

National Association for the Education of Young Children. (1985). *In whose hands? A demographic fact sheet on child care providers.* Washington, DC: Author.

National Center for Children in Poverty. (1991). *Developing family day care resources for low-income families.* New York: Columbia University School of Public Health.

Nelson, M. K. (1988). Providing family day care: An analysis of home-based work. *Social Problems, 35,* 78–94.

Nelson, M. K. (1989). Negotiating care: Relationships between family daycare providers and mothers. *Feminist Studies, 15,* 7–33.

Nelson, M. K. (1990). Mothering others' children: The experiences of family day-care providers. *Signs: Journal of Women in Culture and Society, 15,* 586–605.

Nelson, M. K. (1991a). Mothering others' children: The experiences of family day care providers. In E. Abel & M. Nelson (Eds.), *Circles of care: Work and identity in women's lives* (pp. 210–232). Albany, NY: State University of New York Press.

Nelson, M. K. (1991b). A study of family day care providers: Attitudes towards regulation. *Child and Youth Care Forum, 20,* 225–242.

Pence, A. R., & Goelman, H. (1987a). Silent partners: Parents of children in three types of day care. *Early Childhood Research Quarterly, 2,* 103–118.

Pence, A. R., & Goelman, H. (1987b). Who cares for the child in day care? An examination of caregivers from three types of care. *Early Childhood Research Quarterly, 2,* 315–334.

Pence, A. R., & Goelman, H. (1991). The relationship of regulation, training, and motivation to quality of care in family day care. *Child and Youth Care Forum, 20,* 83–101.

Perreault, J. (1985). *Why people become family day care providers.* Unpublished paper. Atlanta, GA: Save the Children.

Peters, D. L. (1972). *Day care homes: A Pennsylvania profile* (Report No. PSU–CHSD–R–18). University Park, PA: Pennsylvania State University, College of Human Development. (ERIC Document Reproduction Service No. ED 097 097)

Phillips, D., Lande, J., & Goldberg, M. (1990). The state of child care regulation: A comparative analysis. *Early Childhood Research Quarterly, 5,* 151–179.

Pine, B. (1975). *Family day care: A cooperative extension pilot program* (Report No. USDA–CA–12–05–300–211). State University of New York, College of Human Ecology. (ERIC Document Reproduction Service No. ED 124 285)

Poresky, R. B. (1977). *Evaluation report of the pilot project to evaluate effectiveness of utilizing licensed day care home providers as trainers of potential day care home providers.* Manhattan, KS: Kansas State University, Department of Family and Child Development. (ERIC Document Reproduction Service No. ED 154 938)

Powell, D. (1989). *Families and early childhood programs.* Washington, DC: National Association for the Education of Young Children.

Powell, D. R. (1980). *Finding child care: A study of parents' search processes.* Detroit, MI: The Merrill-Palmer Institute.

Prescott, E., Kritchevsky, S., & Jones, E. (1972). *The day care inventory.* Washington, DC: U.S. Department of Health, Education, and Welfare.

Radin, N. (1970). *Evaluation of the daycare consultation program 1969–1970.* Ann Arbor, MI: Michigan University, School of Social Work. (ERIC Document Reproduction Service No. ED 047 331)

Rapp, G. S., & Lloyd, S. A. (1989). The role of "Home as Haven" ideology in child care use. *Family Relations, 38,* 426–430.

Rauch, M. D., & Crowell, D. C. (1974). *Toward high quality family day care for infants and toddlers.* Rockville, MD: National Institute of Mental Health. (ERIC Document Reproduction Service No. ED 110 183)

Raven, M. (1981). The effects of childminding: How much do we know? *Child: Care, Health, and Development, 7,* 103–111.

Read, M., & LaGrange, A. (1990). *Those who care: A report on approved family day care home providers in Alberta.* Red Deer, AB: Child Care Matters.

Richardson, G., & Marx, E. (1989). *A welcome to every child—How France achieves quality in child care: Practical ideas for the United States.* New York: The French-American Foundation.

Rose, S. (1976). *Independent family day care mothers in the Black community.* Unpublished doctoral dissertation, Columbia University Teachers College, New York.

Rosenthal, M. K. (1988). *Attitudes and behaviors of caregivers in family day care: The effects of personal background, professional support system and the immediate caregiving environment.* The Hebrew University of Jerusalem. (ERIC Document Reproduction Service No. ED 306 040)

Rosenthal, M. K. (1990). Social policy and its effects on the daily experiences of infants and toddlers in family day care in Israel. *Journal of Applied Developmental Psychology, 11,* 85–104.

Rosenthal, M. K. (1991). Behaviors and beliefs of caregivers in family day care: The effects of background and work environment. *Early Childhood Research Quarterly, 6,* 263–283.

Rothstein-Fisch, C., & Howes, C. (1988). Toddler-peer interaction in mixed-age groups. *Journal of Applied Developmental Psychology, 9,* 211–218.

Rothschild, M. S. (1978). *Public school center versus family home day care: Single parents' reasons for selection.* Unpublished master's thesis. San Diego State University, San Diego, CA. (ERIC Document Reproduction Service No. ED 162 759)

Rubin, S. (1974). *Home visiting with family day care providers: A report of research conducted with seven Massachusetts' family day care systems.* (ERIC Document Reproduction Service No. ED 102 010)

Rubin, S. (1975). Home visiting with family providers. *Child Welfare, 54,* 645–657.

Ruopp, R., Travers, J., Glantz, F., & Coelen, C. (1979). *Children at the center: Executive summary of the National Day Care Study.* Cambridge, MA: Abt Associates.

Sale, J. S. (1973a). Family day care: One alternative in the delivery of developmental services in early childhood. *American Journal of Orthopsychiatry, 43*(1), 37–45.

Sale, J. S. (1973b). Family day care—A valuable alternative. *Young Children, 28*(4), 209–215.

Sale, J. S. (1984). Family day care homes. In J. Greenman & R.W. Fuqua (Eds.), *Making day care better* (pp. 21–43). New York: Teachers College Press.

Sale, J. S. (1985, September). *Who benefits from child care: A provider's perspective.* Paper presented at the annual meeting of the American Psychological Association, Los Angeles, CA.

Sibley, A. S., & Abbott-Shim, M. A. (1987). *Assessment profile for family day care.* Atlanta, GA: Quality Assistance.

Sibley, A. S., & Abbott-Shim, M. A. (1989). *Study guide for the assessment profile for family day care*. Atlanta, GA: Quality Assistance.

Snow, C. W. (1982). In-service day care training programs: A review and analysis. *Child Care Quarterly, 11*(2), 108–121.

Sonenstein, F., & Wolf, D. (1991). Satisfaction with child care: Perspectives of welfare mothers. *Journal of Social Issues, 37,* 15–31.

Squibb, B. (1986). *The dynamics of family day care: A review of the research*. Unpublished paper.

Squibb, B. (1989). *Interest in training of Maine child caregivers*. Unpublished paper.

Stallings, J. A. (1981, April). *A description of caregivers and children in family day care homes*. Paper presented at the biennial meeting of the Society for Research in Child Development, Boston, MA. (ERIC Document Reproduction Service No. ED 210 087)

Steinberg, L. D., & Green, C. (1979). *How parents may mediate the effect of day care*. (ERIC Document Reproduction Service No. ED 168 698)

Stentzel, C. (1985). *Child care fact sheet: Working mothers and children*. Washington, DC: National Commission on Working Women.

Stith, S., & Davis, A. (1984). Employed mothers and family day-care substitute caregivers: A comparative analysis of infant care. *Child Development, 55,* 1340–1348.

Ungaretti, T. (1987). *The relationship between family day care providers' participation in a college training program and the quality of their child care*. Unpublished paper.

Vartuli, S. (1989, April). *Family day care provider training and assessment*. Paper presented at the biennial meeting of the Society for Research in Child Development, Kansas City, MO.

Waite, L., Leibowitz, A., & Witsberger, C. (1991). What parents pay for: Child care characteristics, quality, and costs. *Journal of Social Issues, 37,* 33–48.

Wandersman, L. P. (1978). An ecological study of the interaction of caregivers' own day care children in family day care homes. *Cornell Journal of Social Relations, 13,* 75–90.

Wandersman, L. P. (1981). Ecological relationships in family day care. *Child Care Quarterly, 10*(2), 89–102.

Washburn, P. V., & Washburn, J. S. (1985). The four roles of the family day care provider. *Child Welfare, 64*(5), 547–553.

Wattenberg, E. (1977). Characteristics of family day care providers: Implications for training. *Child Welfare, 56*(4), 211–228.

Wattenberg, E. (1980). Family day care: Out of the shadows and into the spotlight. *Marriage and Family Review, 3,* 35–62.

Whitebook, M., & Granger, R. (1989). Assessing teacher turnover. *Young Children, 44*(4), 11–14.

Whitebook, M., Howes, C., & Phillips, D. (1989). *Who cares? Child care teachers and the quality of care in America*. Executive Summary, National Child Care Staffing Study. Oakland, CA: Child Care Employee Project.

Willer, B., Hofferth, S., Kisker, E., Divine-Hawkins, P., Farquhar, E., & Glantz, F. (1991). *The demand and supply of child care in 1990*. Washington, DC: National Association for the Education of Young Children.

Willner, M. (1969). Unsupervised family day care in New York City. *Child Welfare, 48,* 342–347.

Willner, M. (1971). Family day care: An escape from poverty. *Social Work, 16,* 30–35.

Winget, M., Winget, F. G., & Popplewell, J. F. (1982). Including parents in evaluating family day care homes. *Child Welfare, 61,* 195–205.

Wolfgang, C. (1977). *Needs assessment study for Franklin County Welfare Department Social Services*. Ohio State University. (ERIC Document Reproduction Service No. ED 180 584)

Zinsser, C. (1990). *Born and raised in east urban: A community study of informal and unregulated child care*. New York: Center for Public Advocacy Research, Inc.

Index

A

Abbot-Shim 39, 47, 51, 60, 113
activities
  informal 14, 66, 67
  pre-planned 64
Adams 1, 8, 63, 96, 104
adult-child ratio 7, 13, 26, 27, 28, 29
advantage, taking, parents 52, 88
affect
  negative 19, 21, 22
  positive 21, 22
affordability 5, 7, 8, 11, 157, 158, 177
Aguirre 17, 50, 51, 55, 143
Anderson 103, 110
assistance, technical 101, 102, 139, 140, 152, 158, 159
Atkinson 48, 52, 75, 76, 77, 82, 87

B

Banspach 17
Bellm 129
Belsky 29, 30, 142
Bollin 38, 39, 40, 46, 48, 51, 52, 53, 54, 55, 56, 57, 61, 64, 142
Bookstein 29, 74
Broberg 29, 74
Brown 129
Brownlee 24, 26
Bryant 6, 38, 39, 43, 48, 51, 78, 80, 85, 86, 89
Bureau of the Census 5

C

California Child Care Initiative 139, 149, 159
California Resource and Referral Network 1
care
  center-based 1, 4, 5, 6, 7, 8, 10, 43, 66, 73, 74, 77, 78, 82, 83, 98, 153, 157,
158, 159
  in-home 4, 5, 7, 25, 82
  relative 4, 6
Caruso 101
Child Development Associate Credential 110, 111, 112, 114, 115, 118, 139, 156
  certification 93
Child Abuse Registry 95
Child Care Food Program 47, 61, 94
Child Care Partnership of Dallas 110
childminding 6, 43, 48, 51, 55, 78, 79, 80, 85, 88, 89
children, in school all day or out of the home 39
Children's Defense Fund 96
Children's Foundation 3, 4, 91, 93, 94, 95, 96, 98, 109
Clarke-Stewart 23, 24, 25, 27, 31, 32, 33, 74
Class 10, 96, 97, 98, 109
Clifford 29, 30, 68, 135
Coelen 10
cognitive skills. See *skill development, cognitive*
Cohen 1, 95, 144, 154, 164
Colbert 121, 133, 134, 135, 138
conflict and strain 66
Corsini 101, 156
cost. See *economics*
Council for Early Childhood Professional Recognition 110
Cox 38, 39, 40, 46, 47, 48, 61
Crowe 129, 132, 135, 137, 138
Crowell 130, 133
Culkin 11
custodial care 10, 78

D

Davis 21
Day Care Environment Inventory 30
"detached attachment" 66

developmental outcome 13, 34
developmentally appropriate/inappropriate practices 18, 66, 155
Direct Assessment 111
directiveness 25
Divine-Hawkins 8, 16, 18, 19, 20, 21, 35, 38, 42, 43, 47, 50, 55, 59, 62, 64, 73, 74, 76, 77, 81, 82, 109, 142
Dunn 26, 30, 31

E

economics 4, 6, 7, 11, 43, 55, 63, 71, 81, 82, 97, 101, 114, 117, 118, 137, 144, 158
Eheart 17, 18, 38, 39, 40, 42, 46, 48, 50, 51, 52, 56, 61, 64, 87, 143
Emlen 8, 38, 39, 40, 42, 51, 52, 60, 62, 75, 81, 87, 89
Enarson 8, 109, 110
Enos 121, 133, 134, 135, 138

F

family day care homes, large 3, 17
Family Day Care Licensing Study 93, 94
family day care providers
  "modernized" 143
  "novice" 144
  "traditional" 143, 144
  "transitional" 144
Family Day Care Rating Scale 28, 29, 30, 68, 69, 70, 71, 135, 136, 137
Family Day Home Care Provider Program 129
Federal Interagency Day Care Regulations 67
Fiene 69
fine motor skills. See *skill development, fine motor*
Fischer 38, 39, 40, 42, 45, 46,

168 FAMILY DAY CARE: OUT OF THE SHADOWS AND INTO THE LIMELIGHT

47, 48, 50, 61, 64, 68, 69, 109, 142
Fisher 39, 40, 49
flexible hours 5, 77, 82
Floge 89
floor of quality 116
Fosburg 16, 17, 35, 38, 47, 55, 59, 62, 64, 142
Frodi 29, 74
funding 1, 93, 130, 158, 159
Fuqua 6, 62, 75, 76, 77, 78, 79

G

games, structured 15
Garduque 13, 19
Glantz 4, 5, 10, 61, 62, 63, 64
Goelman 13, 38, 42, 43, 44, 46, 47, 48, 51, 52, 56, 61, 64, 68, 69, 74, 75, 76, 77, 81, 82
Goldberg 10, 91, 94, 109
Golden 24, 26
Goldsmith 129, 130, 133
good mothers 10
Gordon 5
Gramley 38, 65, 66, 67
Granger 55
Green 75, 82
Greenspan 121
Griffin 146
gross motor skills. See *skill development, gross motor*
group contact, positive 17
group homes 3
group size 3, 11, 21, 23, 27, 28, 29, 34, 61, 67, 91, 94, 104, 105, 106, 107, 109, 155, 157
Gruber 24, 31, 32, 33

H

Harms 29, 30, 68, 135
Harris 6
Harrold 101
Hayes 7
help-giving 25, 83, 84
Hofferth 3, 4, 5, 7, 62
home setting, familiarity of 5, 9, 88, 153
housework 21, 22, 25, 66
Howes 10, 19, 21, 22, 25, 26,
27, 28, 29, 30, 31, 32, 33, 55, 66, 68, 73, 121, 130, 135, 146, 155
Hughes 83, 84, 88
Hult 29, 74
Hwang 29, 74

I

infants and toddlers 23, 30, 34, 104, 114, 155
information, sources of, for providers 78, 106
Innes 16, 17, 18
interactions, child-caregiver 11, 14, 16, 18, 21, 22, 25, 26, 58, 70, 113, 138
interactions, negative 87
Inwald 17

J

Johnson 14, 16, 18
Jones 30, 39, 45, 46, 50, 52, 54, 130, 133, 134, 135, 143

K

Kahn 3, 4, 5, 6, 7, 91
Kamerman 3, 4, 5, 6, 7, 91
Kaplan 133, 134
Kaufman 39, 47, 51, 60
Keeling 68, 135
Kilmer 130, 133, 137, 138
Kisker 5, 6, 7, 38, 40, 61, 62, 79, 81, 82, 157
Kivikink 5, 7, 76
Knuth 23, 27, 30, 31, 142
Kontos 24, 26, 27, 30, 31, 32, 38, 39, 42, 44, 45, 46, 47, 52, 54, 56, 57, 61, 62, 64, 68, 70, 73, 88, 129, 130, 131, 133, 135, 137, 138, 146, 152
Kritchevsky 30
Kuhlthau 6

L

Labensohn 6, 62, 75, 77, 78, 79
LaGrange 50
Lamb 23, 27, 29, 30, 31, 74
Lande 10, 91, 94, 109
language. See *skill development, language*

Lawrence 129, 137, 139, 140, 149, 152, 158
Leavitt 17, 18, 38, 39, 40, 42, 46, 48, 50, 51, 52, 56, 61, 64, 84, 85, 86, 87, 88, 101, 104, 110, 143
Leibowitz 67
Lloyd 75, 76, 79, 82
Local Advisory Team 112
location of family day care home 5, 10, 20, 21, 40, 49, 71, 77, 81, 82, 90, 144
Long 13, 19
Louise Child Care 110
low-wage subsidy 63

M

Machida 121, 132, 133, 134, 146
Majeed 51, 55, 61, 75, 81
Mansfield 46
Marshall 121, 129, 132, 133, 134, 138
Marx 156
Mason 6
Maynard 5
medical exam 107
Meisels 130, 133, 134, 135
Melnick 69, 101
Modigliani 1, 43, 66, 110, 144, 145, 154, 156, 157, 158, 164, 165
Morgan 10, 93, 95, 96, 97, 98, 99, 101, 103, 104, 109, 110
Morris 11, 63
Moss 39, 51, 55, 76, 78, 80, 81, 88
motivation, extrinsic/intrinsic 117, 144, 145

N

National Association for Family Day Care 110, 112, 113, 114, 117, 118, 156
National Association for the Education of Young Children 8, 11, 38, 39, 42
National Center for Children in Poverty 1
National Child Care Supply and Needs Study 4, 6, 81
National Commission on

INDEX 169

Working Women 55
National Day Care Home Study 8, 10, 16, 18, 20, 21, 35, 36, 37, 38, 39, 40, 41, 43, 50, 51, 55, 59, 60, 61, 62, 64, 74, 76, 77, 142, 157
National Longitudinal Survey of Youth 7, 67
Nelson, 35, 50, 51, 55, 63, 76, 81, 82, 86, 106, 107, 109, 110, 153, 157
networking 43, 45, 58, 69, 103, 117, 144, 159
New York Infant Day Care Study 24, 26
Newton 6

P

Palmer 7
Peabody Picture Vocabulary Test 30
Pence 38, 42, 43, 44, 46, 47, 48, 51, 52, 56, 61, 64, 68, 74, 75, 76, 77, 81, 82, 146
Peters 13, 14, 16, 17, 18, 19, 47, 50, 64, 143, 146
Phillips 3, 4, 5, 10, 55, 91, 94, 96, 98, 109, 146, 155
Pine 129, 132, 133, 134, 135, 137
play
  materials 14, 15, 16, 17, 22, 26, 31, 43, 163
  peer 23, 24, 25, 26, 27, 30
  sociodramatic 14, 16, 17
Policare 26
Popplewell 102
Poresky 121, 133, 134, 135
Powell 79, 159
Prescott 30
Professional Preparation Program 111, 112
Profile of Child Care Studies 4, 42, 61

R

Radin 133, 135
Rapp 75, 76, 79, 82
Rauch 133
Read 50, 146
resource and referral services 79, 139, 140, 152
Richardson 156
Richarz 38, 39, 40, 46, 47, 48, 61
Riessen 54, 57, 64, 152
Riley 63
Rodgers 63
Rose 38, 52
Rosenbluth 26
Rosenthal 17, 18, 19, 22, 26, 30, 31, 32, 38, 39, 46, 51, 52, 61, 70, 101, 142, 156
Rothschild 81, 82
Rothstein-Fisch 25, 26
Rubenstein 27, 28
Rubin 121, 132
Ruopp 10

S

Sakai 66, 155
Sale 8, 62, 66, 68, 135, 155
Schell 5, 7, 76
Schieck 6, 76, 79
self-certification 93
Sibley 113
skill development
  cognitive 23, 24, 25, 30, 32, 76, 81, 111
  fine motor 16
  gross motor 15, 16, 21, 26, 31, 32
  language 16, 21, 22, 24, 26, 30, 68, 76, 81
  social 19, 21, 23, 24, 25, 27, 29, 30, 76, 111, 138
Smock 133, 134
social bids, toddler 19, 142
social skills. See *skill development, social*
Sonenstein 5, 6, 7
space, child-designed 22, 23
space requirements 95
Squibb 33, 48, 50
Stallings 20, 21
Steinberg 75, 82
Sternberg 23, 27, 30, 31, 142
Stewart 29, 30, 31, 32, 33, 68, 73
Stith 21
Strain 5
stress 21, 29, 32, 33, 45, 54, 55, 57, 71
supervision of providers 22, 23, 70, 96, 101, 156

T

teaching 16, 21, 25, 66, 71, 138, 142, 155
television viewing 10, 14, 16, 18, 21, 48, 64, 69, 83
Texas Agricultural Extension Service 129
Thompson 17
Titus 129, 132, 135
toy-lending libraries 129
Toy Resource Center 144
toys. See *play materials*
Travers 10

U

Ungaretti 130, 135

V

Vartuli 129, 132, 133, 134, 138, 139
verbal contact 14, 25, 138

W

wages 11, 158
Waite 157
Walker 29, 30, 142
Wandersman 16, 17, 18, 22, 27
Wattenberg 2, 93, 94, 129
Wells 88
Whitebook 10, 55, 146, 155
Whitehead 54
Willer 4, 42, 46, 61, 62, 63, 76, 79, 81, 91
Willner 8, 75, 78, 82
Winget 75, 77, 78, 102
Wisensale 101
Wissoker 7
Witsberger 67
Wolf 5, 6, 7, 75
Woodman 16

Z

Zaslow 7
Zinsser 82, 85, 109, 119, 157